SMART SKILLS: COMMUNICATIONS

SMART SKILLS: COMMUNICATIONS

Turning Words into Results

PATRICK FORSYTH

Legend Press Ltd, 107-111 Fleet Street, London, EC4A 2AB
info@legend-paperbooks.co.uk | www.legendpress.co.uk

Contents © Patrick Forsyth 2019

Print ISBN 978-1-78955-001-6
Ebook ISBN 978-1-78955-000-9
Set in Times. Printing managed by Jellyfish Solutions Ltd.
Cover design by Linnet Mattey | www.linnetmattey.com

CONTENTS

FOREWORD

This is the fourth book that Patrick Forsyth has written for Legend Business Books' *Smart Skills* series. The subject matter of the new title, *Communications*, is fundamental to all business success, as well as the activities of business writing, meetings and persuasion addressed in his three previous books and to other titles in the series.

Patrick himself has a talent for communicating sound behavioural advice, grounded in personal experience with jargon-free clarity, which is immediately understandable. After identifying the foundations of success in communication and the virtues of preparation, the author moves on to apply his general principles to specific activities: communicating face-to-face, the various forms of business communication, making presentations, being persuasive and bringing together all the skills to negotiate successfully.

This new addition to the *Smart Skills* is for all business people: in mid-career, self-employed or entering the commercial world for the first time. Readers with some time in business will relate Patrick Forsyth's advice to their own experience and will recognise along the way their own communications shortcomings. I wish that this book had been around when I started out in business many years ago.

Jonathan Reuvid

INTRODUCTION

One should not aim at being possible to understand, but at being impossible to misunderstand.

Marcus Fabius Quintillian

We all communicate much of the time, and the workplace is no exception. We do so for all sorts of reasons, for instance to:

- Inform
- Instruct
- Prompt action
- Persuade
- Motivate
- Change opinions
- Prompt debate or discussion
- Stimulate the generation of ideas
- Build on prior contacts or thinking

Often all goes well. Often we hardly think about it. Indeed how difficult is it to say: *What time do you call this?* to the postman or ask for a salary increase, or make a presentation to the Board?

Well, leaving aside the postman, the answer may be not only that such things can be difficult, but also that when they are poorly executed problems are not far behind. In most workplaces you do not have to eavesdrop for long to hear the immediate results of poor communication: *But I thought you said … You should have said … What!?* Similarly, failing to get your point across at a meeting or making a lacklustre presentation can change the course of subsequent events to your detriment. Today we also have a plethora of ever advancing electronic routes for communication to get to grips with and use effectively.

There are challenges: for instance, those making a poor presentation often cite lack of time to prepare as an excuse. More often than some recognisable fault destroying or diluting the effectiveness of communications, it is *lack* of any thought that jeopardises it. It is assumed all will be well and no great thought or preparation occurs.

This is dangerous because the fact is that communication is often *not* easy, indeed a host of factors combine to create difficulties. For example, think about this: how quickly and easily could you tell someone who doesn't already know how to tie a necktie? And no, you cannot demonstrate – words only.

This book addresses these problems: how to overcome difficulties, how to deal with specific modes of communication – for instance making a presentation or writing documents – and overall it highlights the *opportunities* that good communication produces. This is key. The reason to take any sort of interest in how communication works is because of the results good, accurate and clear communications can achieve. How you communicate also affects how you are seen: it creates a profile, for good or ill, and enhances (or otherwise) reputations.

Two further things: first, with limited space individual chapters here have a tight focus, but include points used in context of their particular method or type of communication that may have relevance elsewhere in this *Smart Skills* series. Hence, for example, a point about face-to-face communication may be useful when considering presentations. Similarly, the chapter about the overall aspects of preparations is designed to be relevant to any kind of communication. Secondly, the book is intended to be useful whatever role someone may have and whoever they communicate with and how they do it – communicating is a *career* skill (influencing how you fare in the workplace) as well as a necessary work one.

There is a need to take it seriously, but that said, the communications process is essentially common sense and the thinking that reading this book can prompt is designed to make your communications more likely to be effective and achieve what you want.

Note: Let's get to a specific lesson immediately. What about *political correctness*? Someone took me to task recently about using the expression "manning the office". I think this makes a point: you can take this sort of thing too far. After all the suggested alternative "staffing the office" means something different. It usually means recruiting people to work in the office, whereas "manning the office" normally refers to the process of who is on duty at what time, shifts and so on.

That said, even if you want to say "ridiculous" occasionally, this is an area for some care. Any references to gender, sexuality, religion, political opinion and so on, must be checked, first to see if it is necessary and secondly to make sure that if so the message is delivered with suitable sensitivity. In the meantime I shall try to practice what I preach as we go on.

CHAPTER 1

THE FOUNDATION OF SUCCESS

"Please be sure to lock your door securely before entering or leaving your room."

Notice on the inside of a hotel bedroom door.

The notice quoted above makes a good point. Someone wrote that, printed it and put on 252 doors and still didn't notice that it was nonsense – and it is just one sentence. How many times have you heard someone in your office say something like: *But I thought you said...*? What is the difference between saying something is: *quite nice* and *rather nice*? And would you find anything that only warranted either description the least bit interesting?

Make no mistake: communication can be difficult.

Have you ever come out of a meeting or put the telephone down on someone and said to yourself: *what's the matter with that idiot, don't they understand anything*? And, if so, did it cross your mind afterwards that maybe the difficulty was that you were not explaining matters as well as you could? Make no mistake: the responsibility for making communication work lies primarily with the communicator.

The first rule about communication is never to assume

it is simple. It is easy to take communicating for granted; indeed much of it *is* straightforward. But sometimes we are not as precise as we might be; never mind, often we muddle through and little harm is done. Except that occasionally it is. Some communication breakdowns become out and out derailments.

Often there is so much hanging on it that communications must be got right and the penalties of not so doing range from minor disgruntlement to, at worst, a cessation of business. So the rule – everyone needing to take responsibility for their communication and to execute it in a sufficiently considered manner to make it work effectively – is a vital one.

THE DIFFICULTIES

Any difficulties occur not because other people are especially perverse but because communication is, in fact, *inherently difficult*. Let's consider why.

Inherent problems

To communicate successfully, it is necessary to make sure people:

- Hear what you say, and thus listen.
- Understand, and do so accurately.
- Agree, certainly with most of it, and take action if that is intended.
- Are stimulated to provide feedback.

Consider the areas above in turn in the context of the inherent way in which human nature works:

Objective: to hear/listen (or read).

Difficulties:
- People cannot or will not concentrate for long periods of time, so this fact must be accommodated by the way we communicate. Long monologues are out, written communication should have plenty of breaks, headings and fresh starts, and two way conversation must be used to prevent people thinking they are pinned down and have to listen to something interminable.
- People pay less attention to elements of a communication that appear to them unimportant, so creating the right emphasis, to ensure that key points are not missed, is the responsibility of the communicator.

In other words you have to work at making sure you are heard – to earn a hearing.

Objective: to ensure accurate understanding.

Difficulties:
- People make assumptions based on their past experience, so you must make sure you relate to just that. If you wrongly assume certain experience exists then your message will not make much sense (imagine trying to teach someone to drive if they had never sat in a car: *press your foot on the accelerator – what's that?*).
- Other peoples' jargon is often not understood, so think very carefully about the amount you use and with whom. Jargon is "professional slang" and creates a useful shorthand between people in the know, for example in one organisation or one industry, but dilutes a message if used inappropriately. For instance, used in a way that assumes a greater competence than actually exists (and remember, people don't like to sound stupid and may well be reluctant to say, *I don't understand*) it will hinder understanding.

- Things heard but not seen are more easily misunder- stood, thus anything you can show may be useful; so too are words "painting a picture."
- Assumptions are often drawn before a speaker finishes: the listener is, in fact, saying to themselves, *I'm sure I can see where this is going* and their concentration reduces, focusing instead on planning their own next comment. This too needs accommodating and where a point is key, feedback should be sought to ensure that concentration has not faltered and the message really has got through.

Overall, clarity not only allows people to understand what is put to them, it allows them to agree with the sense of it too.

Objective: obtain agreement and prompt action.

Difficulties:
Changing habits is difficult: recognising this is the first step to influencing it. A stronger case may need making than would be the case if this was not true. It also means that care must be taken to link past and future, for example not saying: *that was wrong and this is better* but rather: *that was fine then, but this will be better in future* (and explaining how changed circumstances make this so). Any phraseology that casts doubt on someone's early decisions should be avoided wherever possible.

There may be fear of taking action – *will it work? What will people think? What will my boss think? What are the consequences of it not working out?* This risk avoidance is a natural feeling: recognising this and offering appropriate reassurance is vital.

Many people are simply reluctant to make decisions: they may need real help from you and it is a mistake to assume that laying out an irresistible case and just waiting for commitment is all there is to it.

In addition, you need a further objective:

Objective: stimulating feedback.

Difficulties:
- Some (all?) people sometimes deliberately hide their reaction – some flushing out and reading between the lines may be necessary
- Appearances can be deceptive. For example, *Trust me* is as often a warning sign as a comment to be welcomed – some care is necessary.

The net effect of all this is rather like trying to peer through fog. Communication goes to and fro, but effectively through a filter, part of which may be blocked, perhaps warped or let through only incompletely. Partly, the remedy to all this is simply watchfulness. If you appreciate the difficulties, you can adjust your communications style a little to compensate, and thus achieve better understanding.

One moral is surely clear. Communication is likely to be better for some planning. This may only be a few second's thought – the old premise of engaging the brain before the mouth (or writing arm) through to making some notes before you draft an email or proposal, or even sitting down with a colleague for a while to thrash out the best way to approach something.

Already this provides some antidotes to the inherent difficulties, but are there any principles that run parallel and provide mechanisms to balance the difficulty and make matters easier? Luckily the answer is: yes there are.

AIDS TO GOOD COMMUNICATION

Good communication is, in part, a matter of attention to detail. Just using one word instead of another can make a slight difference. Actually, using words with precision can make a *significant* difference. And there are plenty of other factors that contribute, many explored as this book continues. But there are also certain overall factors that are of major influence and which can be used to condition your communications. These include:

The *What about me?* factor

Any message is more likely to be listened to and accepted if how it affects people is spelt out. Whatever the effect, people want to know, *What do I gain from this*? and *How will it hurt me?* People are interested in both the potential positive and negative effects. Tell someone that you have a new, reorganised system and they will likely think the worst. Certainly their reaction is unlikely to be simply, *Good for you*, it is more likely to be, *Sounds like that will be complicated* or *Bet that will have teething troubles or slow things down*. Tell them they are going to get a faster, more certain result with the new system, and add that it is already drawing good reactions and you spell out the message and what the effects on them will be altogether, rather than leaving them asking questions.

Whatever you say, bear in mind that people view it in this kind of way, build in the answers and you avert their potential suspicion and make them more likely to want to take the message on board.

The *That's logical* factor

The sequence and structure of communication is very important. If people know what it is, understand why it was chosen and believe it will work *for them*, then they will pay more attention. Conversely, if it is unclear or illogical then they worry about it, and this takes their mind off listening.

Information is remembered and used in an order – try saying your own telephone number as quickly backwards as you do forwards – so your selection of a sensible order for communication will make sense to people and again they will warm to the message.

Telling people about this is called signposting. Say, *Let me give you some details about the specification, the performance and the installation* and, provided that makes sense to the listener, they will want to hear what comes next. So tell them about the specification and then move on. It is almost impossible to overuse signposting. Sometimes order can be strengthened by explaining why the order has been chosen, *Let's go through it chronologically, perhaps I could spell out...*

Whatever you have to say, think about what you say first, second, third and so on and make the order you choose an appropriate sequence.

The *I can relate to that* factor

Imagine a description of a wonderful sunset. What does it make you think of? Well, a sunset, you may say. But how do you do this? You recall sunsets you have seen in the past and what you imagine draws on that memory, probably conjuring up a composite based on many memories. Because it's reasonable to assume that you have previously seen a sunset, and enjoyed the experience, I can be fairly certain that a brief description will put what I want in your mind.

It is, in fact, almost impossible not to allow related things to come into your mind as you take in a message (try it now and *do not* think about a refreshing drink. See.) This fact about the way the human mind works must be allowed for and used to promote clear understanding.

Conversely, if I was to ask you to call to mind, say, the house in which I live and yet don't describe it to you, then this is impossible, unless you have been there or discussed the matter with me previously. All you can do is guess, wildly perhaps, that all authors live in a garret or all authors are rich and live in mansions (both wrong!).

So, with this factor also inherent to communication, it is useful to try to judge carefully peoples' prior experience; or indeed to ask about it. You may also refer to it with phrases linking what you are saying to the experience of the other person. For example, saying things like *This is like... You will remember...– Do you know...? This is similar, but...* are all designed to help the listener grasp what you are saying more easily and more accurately.

Beware of getting at cross purposes because you assume someone has a frame of reference for something which they do not; link to their experience and use it to reinforce your message.

The *Again and again* factor

Repetition is a fundamental help in grasping a point. Repetition is a fundamental help in... Sorry; it is true, but it does not imply just repeatedly saying the same thing, in the same words. Repetition takes a number of forms:

- Things repeated in different ways (or at different stages of the same conversation).
- Points made in more than one manner: for example, being spoken and written down.
- Using summaries or checklists to recap key points.
- Reminders over a period of time (maybe varying the method: phone, email or meeting).

This can be overdone (as in the introduction to this point here), but it is also a genuinely valuable aid to getting the message across, especially when used with the other factors now mentioned. People really are more likely to retain what they take in more than once. Enough repetition, now to the details of preparation.

CHAPTER 2

PREPARING TO COMMUNICATE

The ability to express an idea
Is well nigh as important as the idea itself.

Bernard Baruch

Enough has been said about the difficulties of communicating effectively to demonstrate that anything and everything that helps it go well is worth considering. Here we go further and consider elements that are absolute fundamentals in getting it right. Beyond the universal advice provided, there is a necessity to adopt specific approaches to specific tasks – writing a report, say, has some unique elements to it.

Note: This chapter is thus linked strongly to others and it may be worthwhile referring back to it as you read other parts of this book.

QUESTIONS AND LISTENING

Both may seem obvious, but require some real consideration and make a good starting point.

The question of questions

Many communication situations need to be clarified by the asking of questions. Unless you know the facts, unless you know what people think and, most importantly, unless you know *why* things are as they are, proceeding further may be difficult or impossible. How do you resolve a dispute without understanding why people are at loggerheads? How do you persuade people to action without knowing how they view the area in which you want them to get involved? How do you motivate without knowing what is important to people or what worries them? The answer is surely "with difficulty". Questions create involvement, they get people talking and the answers they prompt provide the foundation for much of what makes communication successful.

But questioning is more than just blurting out the first thing that comes to mind – *why do you say that?* – as even a simple phrase may carry overtones and people wonder if you are suggesting they should not have said something, or if you see no relevance for the point made.

Additionally, many questions can easily be ambiguous. It's all too easy to ask something that, only because it is loosely phrased, prompts an unintended response. Ask, *How long will that take?* and the reply may simply be: *Not long*. Ask, *Will you finish that before the meeting at 11 o'clock?* and you will then be well able to prepare for the meeting.

Beyond simple clarity you need to consider and use three distinctly different kinds of question:

1. Closed questions: these prompt rapid *Yes* or *No* answers, and are useful both as a starting point (they can also be made easy to answer thus easing someone into the questioning process) and to gain rapid confirmation of something. Too many closed questions on the other hand create a virtual monologue in which the questioner seems to be doing most of the talking, and this can be annoying or unsatisfying to the other person.

2. Open questions: these *cannot* be answered with a simple *Yes* or *No* and typically begin with words like: *what, where, why, how, who*, and *when* and phrases such as *Tell me about ....* They get people talking and involve them. By prompting fuller answers and explanations they also produce far more information than closed questions.

3. Probing questions: these are a series of linked questions designed to pursue a point: thus a second question, *What else is important about...* or a phrase like: *Tell me more about...* get people to fill out a picture and can thus produce both more detail and the "why" which lies beyond more superficial answers.

Many a communication is made to succeed by the simple prerequisite of starting with some questions.

It is important to give sufficient time to any necessary questioning process. It may also be important to make it clear to others that you *are* giving the process sufficient time. This may indicate, say, the importance with which something is regarded; the reverse may give the wrong impression – indicating a lack of concern. Both may be important. This is something that it may sometimes be useful to spell out: *I want to go through this thoroughly, I can take an hour or so now and if that proves inadequate we can come back to it. Let's see how we get on.*

Listening skills

Do not look back, but can you remember the three different categories of question just mentioned? If not (and be honest) then consider that the principle is similar – without

22

concentration we do not take in every detail of what we are reading, or hearing.

The key thing then is to regard listening as an *active* process. It is something we all need to work at. What does this mean? There are perhaps a surprising amount of ways to improve your listening – and the retention of information, including details crucial to understanding. These include the need to:

- *Want to listen:* This is easy once you realise how useful it is to do so.
- *Look like a good listener:* People will appreciate it and if they see they have your attention feedback will be more forthcoming.
- *Understand:* It is not just the words but the meaning that lies behind them you must note.
- *React:* Let people see that you have heard, understood and are interested. Nods, small gestures and signs and comments will encourage the other person's confidence and participation – *right?*
- *Stop talking:* Other than small acknowledgements, you cannot talk and listen at the same time. Do not interrupt.
- *Use empathy:* Put yourself in the other person's shoes and make sure you really appreciate their pointofview.
- *Check:* If necessary, ask questions promptly to clarify matters as the conversation proceeds. An understanding based even partly on guesses or assumptions is dangerous. But ask questions diplomatically; do not say, *You didn't explain that properly.*
- *Remain unemotional:* Too much thinking ahead – *However can I overcome that point?* – can distract you.
- *Concentrate:* Allow nothing to distract you.
- *Look at the other person:* Nothing is read more rapidly as disinterest than an inadequate focus of attention – good eye contact is essential, lack of it risks being read as deviousness.

- *Note particularly key points:* Edit what you hear so that you can better retain key points manageably.
- *Avoid personalities:* Do not let your view of someone as a person distract you from the message.
- *Do not lose yourself in subsequent arguments:* Some thinking ahead may be useful, too much and you suddenly may find you have missed something.
- *Avoid negatives:* To begin with clear signs of disagreement (even a dismissive look) can make the other person clam up and destroy the dialogue.
- *Make notes:* Do not trust your memory, and if it is polite to do so, ask permission before writing their comments down.

Make no mistake, if you listen – *really* listen – then everything that follows will be a little easier and more certain.

PREPARATION: THE ESSENTIALS

Do not think that having to prepare implies some sort of weakness. For instance, the "born" public speaker, effortlessly sailing through their presentation is likely only able to give this impression because they are well prepared. It needs doing, must be done well and done productively. In fact, good preparation should save time overall.

Whether you are to write a report, make a presentation or undertake something simpler like writing an email or a letter, the process is essentially similar. What does change is the complexity and the time preparation takes. To provide an example, the following relates primarily to making a presentation but, whatever is done, *the key approaches always apply.*

Setting objectives

Whatever you may need to communicate and however it is to be done, its purpose must be clear. You must be able to answer the question: *Why am I doing this?* And set out a purpose, one that always needs to involve you and the recipients of your message and describes what effect it should have on them. Remember that communication can have many overall intentions (to inform, motivate and more, described in Chapter 1), and that these are not mutually exclusive. The more different intentions you have, the more preparation to ensure all will be fulfilled.

Objectives need not only to be clear, but spelt out in sufficient detail (certainly in your own mind and sometimes for others). They must act as a genuine guide to what you will do. They also need to reflect not just what you want, but the audience's view also.

Often a much-quoted acronym can provide a good guide here: SMART. This stands for:

- **S**pecific
- **M**easurable
- **A**chievable
- **R**ealistic
- **T**imed.

As an example you might regard objectives linked to your reading Chapter 6, on presentations, so as to:

- Enable you to ensure your presentations come over in future in a way that audiences will find appropriate and informative *(specific)*.
- Ensure *(measurable)* action takes place afterwards (here you might link to any appropriate measure: from agreements or actions that group members take or commit to the volume of applause received!).
- Be right for you: sufficient, understandable information

in manageable form that really allows you to change and improve what you do later (an *achievable* result).

- Be *realistic*, that is desirable – hence a short text (if it took you several days to read, the effort might prove greater than any benefit coming from doing so).
- Provide *timing;* always a good factor to include in any objective. By when are you going to finish reading this chapter? When is your next presentation? How far ahead of it should you prepare?

So, ask yourself whether you are clear in this respect before you even begin to prepare. If you know *why* the presentation must be made, and *what* you intend to *achieve* then you are well on the way to success. Time spent sorting this, and making sure you have a clear vision of what the objectives are, is time well spent. It may only take a few moments or it may need more thought and take more time. So be it; it is worth doing and in any case may well save time on later stages of preparation.

With your purpose clear, and a constant eye, as it were, on the audience, you can begin to assemble your message.

Deciding on the message

There is more to this than simply banging down the points in sequence, something that was hinted at earlier. A more systematic approach is necessary, indeed a more systematic approach can quickly become a habit thus allowing you to deliver what you want promptly and certainly.

The following provides a full description of a tried and tested approach as well as the fullest degree of preparation necessary, but it is important to stress that this is not offered as something that must be followed slavishly. The important thing is to find, experiment with, refine and then use a method that suits *you*. In addition, practice and experience, or other factors such as familiarity with your chosen topic, may well allow you to adopt a "shorthand" version of these approaches that is quicker, but still does the total job that is necessary.

There is a need here to take one point at a time (if only because there is no other way to proceed).

We also need to investigate more about *how* you will put the message across. Both link to the structure involved: what comes first, second and third and what constitutes the beginning, the middle and the ending.

There is something of the chicken and egg here. Does preparation or structure logically come first? Both are important, both are interrelated, the sequence chosen here works well and is intended to show the reader how to put a presentation together as it would need to be done in real life. The details and the sequence can equally apply to something such as writing a report or proposal, and in less elaborate form to much else besides. So, onto the detail of assembling the message.

Putting it together

It is not only necessary to "engage the brain before the mouth", but also vital to think through in advance what a presentation must be. The following process of thinking through and preparation is recommended solely for its practicality and can be adapted to cope with any sort of presentation, of any length or complexity and for any purpose.

Many communications fail or their effectiveness is diluted because preparation is skimped. Accepting that preparation takes time and building this into your work plan is the first step to being a good communicator. In the long run it saves time, in part on the old premise that while there is never time to do things properly, there always has to be time made available to sort out any mess caused by inadequacies.

There are six stages here (described, in part, by continuing the presentations example). The very best way of linking the principles described here to real life is to go through them with some personal project, a pending presentation perhaps, in mind and link this to the approach that follows.

Stage 1: Listing

Forget about everything such as sequence, structure and arrangement; just concentrate on and list – in short note (or keyword) form – every significant point that the presentation might usefully contain. Give yourself plenty of space (something larger than the standard A4 sheet is often useful; this lets you see everything at one glance). Set down the points as they occur to you, almost at random across the page. For something simple this might result only in a dozen words, or it might be far more.

You will find that this is a good thought prompter. It enables you to fill out the picture as one thought leads to another, with the freestyle approach removing the need to pause and try to link points or worry about sequence. With this done, and with some presentations it may only take a short time, you can move on to the next stage with a full picture of the possibilities for the message in front of you.

Stage 2: Sorting

Now, you can review what you have noted down and begin to bring some order to it, deciding:

- What comes first, second and so on.
- What logically links together, and how.
- What provides evidence, example or illustration to the points made.

At the same time, you can – and probably will – add some additional things and have second thoughts about other items, which you will delete, as well as amending the wording a little if necessary. You need to bear in mind here what kind of duration (or length) is required or acceptable.

This stage can often be completed in a short time by simply annotating and amending the first stage document. Using a second colour can make this quick and easy, as do link lines, arrows and other enhancements to your original notes.

At the same time you can begin to catch any more detailed element that comes to mind as you go through (including ways of presenting as well as content), noting what it is at more length on the page or alongside.

Stage 3: Arranging

Sometimes, at the end of stage two, you have a note that is sufficiently clear and from which you can work direct in finalising matters. If it can benefit from clarification however, it may be worth rewriting it as a neat list; or this could be the stage where you type it and put it on screen if you are working digitally and want to be able to print or create a file to share.

Final revision is possible as you do this; certainly you should be left with a list reflecting the content, emphasis, level of detail and so on that you feel is appropriate. You may well find you are pruning a bit to make things more manageable at this stage, rather than searching for more contents and additional points to make.

Stage 4: Reviewing

This may be unnecessary. Sufficient thought may have been brought to bear earlier. However, for something particularly complex or important (or both) it may be worth running a final rule over what you now have down. Sleep on it first perhaps — certainly avoid finalising matters for a moment if you have got too close to it. It is easy to find you cannot see the wood for the trees.

Make any final amendments to the list (if this is on screen

it is a simple matter) and use this as your final "route map" as preparation continues.

Stage 5: Prepare the "message"

In our example this would be speaker's notes (of which more later) – if the job is to write something then this is where you actually write it. Now you can turn your firm intentions about content into something representing not only *what* will be said, but also *how* you will put it over. One of the virtues of the procedure advocated here is that it stops you trying to think about *what* to say and *how* to say it at the same time; it is much easier to take them in turn. This stage must be done carefully, though the earlier work will have helped to make it easier and quicker to get the necessary detail down.

A couple of tips:

- If possible, *choose the right moment*. There seem to be times when words flow more easily than others (and it may help literally to talk it through to yourself as you go through this stage). Certainly interruptions can disrupt the flow and make preparation take much longer, as you recap and restart again and again. The right, uninterrupted time in a comfortable environment will help.
- K*eep going*. By this I mean do not pause and agonize over a phrase, a heading or some other detail. You can always come back to that, indeed it may be easier amend later. If you keep going you maintain the flow, allowing consistent thinking to carry you through the structure to the end so that you can "see" the overall shape of it. Once you have the main detail down then you can go back and fine-tune, adding any final thoughts to complete the picture. The precise format of notes can be very helpful, something that is investigated later.

Stage 6: A final check

A final look (perhaps after a break) is always valuable. This is also the time to consider rehearsal – either talking it through to yourself, to a tape recorder or a friend or colleague, or going through a full scale "dress rehearsal".

Thereafter, depending on the nature of the presentation, it may be useful – or necessary – to spend more time, either in revision or just going over what you plan to do. You should not overdo revision at this stage; however, there comes a time to simply be content you have it right and stick with it. If preparing a written document then it is here that any necessary editing takes place. There will, incidentally, be some editing – few, if any people, write without the need to fine-tune the text to produce a final version.

This whole preparation process is important and not to be skimped. Preparation does get easier however. You will find that, with practice, you begin to produce material that needs less amendment and that both getting it down and the subsequent revision begin to take less time.

At the end of the day, as has been said, you need to find your own version of the procedures set out here. A systematic approach helps, but the intention is not to over-engineer the process. What matters is that you are comfortable that your chosen approach works for you. If this is the case then, provided it remains consciously designed to achieve what is necessary, it will become a habit. It will need less thinking about, yet still act to guarantee that you turn out something that you are content meets the needs, whatever they may be.

Summary

Preparation is a vital part of communicating. At its simplest it is merely a moment's constructive thought. More often more is necessary. The key issues are:

- Always to proceed any thinking by devising a clear objective.
- To prepare messages with a clear idea of what intentions they reflect (informing, persuading, etc.).
- To think matters through systematically and separate deciding *what* you will say (or put over in whatever way), from *how* you will put things and thus the precise language you will use.
- To give this process sufficient time and, if possible, build in some pauses so that you do not become unable to see the wood for the trees.
- To be prepared to fine-tune the message to get it right.

CHAPTER 3

FACE-TO-FACE COMMUNICATIONS

It is only shallow people
who do not judge by appearances.

Oscar Wilde

One of Oscar Wilde's many observations, quoted above, makes a fair warning to any communicator. Certainly face-to-face contact demands a consideration of what is visible, and there is a need to "look the part", as it were.

IMAGE

Appearance inevitably offers clues to what lies behind it: people infer from your appearance and behaviour something about you and your organisation.

Appearance

I would not presume to suggest appropriate dress. But it needs some thought. Fashions come and go and norms are different in different settings and according to the nature of the organisation. Informality is now common, but perhaps should not be overdone – above all you need to look *appropriate*. As an extreme example of how every aspect of appearance may have a bearing, I once met someone in my own business to discuss training who said he had received one proposal, but: *as the consultant arrived here in a Porsche, I thought I should get another quote*.

Alongside how people present themselves, the manner they adopt is important also.

Manner

The criteria again vary, for example customers like it if the people who deal with them are:

- Approachable.
- Friendly, though not initially too informal.
- Clearly focused exclusively on them: customers find it very disconcerting if someone allows interruptions (such as telephone calls, or colleagues) to punctuate their being dealt with and it makes the process take longer.
- Courteous in word and manner, but without it being overdone and becoming grovelling.
- Interested in them, which perhaps contributes more than anything else to an overall manner that customers like.

These points have general relevance and you can think through what is best in terms of who you deal with. Additionally, manner should be individually directed. The forced smile and *Have a nice day* school of customer courtesy is diluted not only from overuse, but because it is mechanistically directed at everyone. If you can build in something that is clearly directed at the individual e.g. *I can see you're in a rush, let me*... then this enhances a pleasing manner still further.

The awful saying that you should *be sincere whether you mean it or not* is the reverse of the truth. People will usually spot insincerity a mile off. If you project a positive attitude and look organised (or whatever other characteristic your role suggests), this will stand you in good stead through many kinds of contact.

BODY LANGUAGE

When you are face-to-face it would be wrong to ignore non-verbal clues to making the communication go well. People project all sorts of unspoken guides as to their feelings. Some are obvious, indeed allowed to show just so that they *are* obvious, as when someone displays clear signs of impatience. Others are less so.

Body language is not an exact science. But it is interesting, provides clues and may be worth some study. One gesture alone is certainly not an infallible sign of anything – there could be external factors you are unaware of – but each should help inform an accurate overall profile.

The checklist that follows is not intended as points cast in stone, more as a guide to what *may* be indicated. The more signs point to the same thing the more certainly you might take on board the message; however, caution is always sensible and you should always bear in mind that, as above, body language offers clues not infallible insights.

Checklist: BODY LANGUAGE CLUES

OPEN MINDEDNESS shown by:
- Open hands
- Unbuttoned coat

WARINESS shown by:
- Arms crossed on chest
- Legs over chair arm while seated
- Sitting in armless chair reversed
- Crossing legs
- Fist-like gestures
- Pointing index finger
- Karate chops

THINKING/ANALYSING shown by:
- Hand to face gestures
- Head tilted
- Stroking chin
- Peering over glasses
- Taking glasses off – cleaning
- Glasses earpiece in mouth
- Getting up from table – walking
- Putting hand to bridge of nose

TERRITORIAL DOMINANCE shown by:
- Feet on desk
- Feet on chair
- Leaning against/touching object
- Placing object in a desired space
- Hands behind head – leaning back

NERVOUSNESS shown by:
- Clearing throat
- Whew sound
- Whistling
- Picking or pinching flesh
- Fidgeting in chair
- Hands covering mouth while speaking
- Lack of eye contact
- Tugging at trousers or skirt while seated
- Jingling money in pockets
- Tugging at ear
- Perspiration/wringing of hands

CONFIDENCE shown by:

- Steepling of the hands
- Hands on back of head – authority position
- Back stiffened
- Hands in coat pockets, with thumbs outside
- Hands on lapels of coat

ACCEPTANCE shown by:

- Hand to chest
- Open arms and hands
- Touching gestures
- Moving closer to another
- Preening

EXPECTANCY shown by:

- Rubbing palms
- Jingling money
- Crossed fingers
- Moving closer

SUSPICION shown by:

- Not looking at you
- Arms crossed

FRUSTRATION shown by:

- Short breaths
- Tutting sound
- Tightly clenched hands
- Wringing hands
- Fist-like gestures
- Pointing index finger
- Running hand through hair
- Rubbing back of neck

BOREDOM shown by:

- Doodling
- Moving away from you
- Silhouette body towards you
- Sideways glance
- Touch/rub nose
- Rubbing eye(s)
- Buttoning coat
- Drawing away

ALERTNESS/ATTENTION shown by:

- Hands on hips
- Hands on mid-thigh when seated
- Sitting on edge of chair
- Arms spread, gripping edge of table/desk
- Moving closer
- Open hands
- Hand to face gestures
- Unbuttoning coat
- Tilted head

Body language is something worth keeping an eye on though it should not become a fixation. After all there are plenty of other things to concentrate on.

That said, when every sign is being read to provide as detailed an impression as possible of who it is that is being dealt with, and what they are like, it is important.

ORGANISATION

It is not only how you look and behave that's important, it's how well-organised you appear.

Organised people

Clearly being well-organised improves efficiency and productivity. Even something as simple as being able to put your hand on the right file speeds up how things can be dealt with. But it is the impression that is given that we are primarily concerned with here. Good organisation speaks of efficiency and gives others confidence in your abilities.

The reverse is easy to understand. Appear disorganised, and maybe also hesitant or unsure, and what you say will to some degree immediately be prejudged and likely given a negative spin. So everything that you do that can send such signals needs to be organised to send signals that shout efficiency. This is true wherever you work. Good organisation sets the scene for good communications, indeed it communicates of itself; the job is to make it say what you want.

Note: Sometimes face-to-face communication involves more than just people talking to each other. For example, you may need to demonstrate something, say a system or product. This may be best set up in advance, prepared, rehearsed if necessary; in other words, you need to take action to ensure it goes well – first time. Problems with this sort of thing always dilute the impression you intend to make. One more major face-to-face situation deserves comment: meetings.

MEETINGS

Meetings are ubiquitous, but they can be hard work, difficult – even boring. Too often they end having served no useful purpose and not advancing matters or prompting decisions . They are however necessary to communication – with staff, clients, whoever – so they must be made to work.

An old saying states that the ideal meeting is two people – with one absent. They are the archetypal mixed blessing. They consume so much time (and thus cost), and yet *are* an important part of organisational communications, consultation, debate and decision making. We need them. Or certainly we need some of them. We must, however, get the most from them, and we do not need too many, or those that are too long nor, above all, those that are unconstructive. What is more, good, effective meetings do not just happen.

No rule says that you must put up with bad ones in order to get an occasional good one thrown in, and nothing will be done to create a culture of effective meetings unless everyone in an organisation actively works at it. Everybody's role is important, whether running a meeting or attending one. So, how can you make them work?

The benefits of meeting

Whatever the meeting, large or small, formal or informal, long or short, whatever its purpose – you can make it go well. Meetings can seek to do a number of things: inform, analyse and solve problems, discuss and exchange views, inspire and motivate, counsel and reconcile conflict, obtain opinion and feedback, persuade, train and develop, reinforce the status quo, impress and progress projects.

You can doubtless extend the list. The key purpose is surely most often to prompt change (it's surely pointless having a meeting if nothing changes), and that means making decisions.

So any meeting has to be constructive and put people in a position where *good* decisions can prompt *appropriate* action.

Furthermore, a good meeting can go further, prompting discussion and action that would never have occurred unless a particular group got together.

Setting up meetings

If a meeting is to be truly successful, then ensuring its success must begin long before it starts – the *I think we're all here, what shall we deal with first?* school of meeting organisation is not recommended.

First, ask some basic questions. For example: why is a meeting necessary? Should it be a regular meeting? Think very carefully about this; once a meeting is designated as being weekly, monthly or whatever it can become a routine that is difficult to break and, at worst, becomes just a regular waste of time. Who should attend? And who should not?

If you are clear in these respects then you can proceed. Some key points to bear in mind include:

- *Setting an agenda:* This is crucial, no meeting will go well if you simply invent the content as you go along (notify the attendees of the agenda in advance and give good notice of contributions required from others).
- *Timing:* Set a start time *and* a finishing time, then you can judge the way to conduct matters alongside the duration and even put some rough timing to individual topics. Respect the timing too: start on time and work to stick with the duration planned.
- *Objective:* Always set a clear objective spelling out *why* a meeting is being held (and the answer should never be: *because it's a month since the last one!)*
- *Prepare yourself:* Read all necessary papers, check all necessary details and think about how you will handle

both your own contribution and the stimulation, and control, of others'.

- *Insist others prepare also:* This may mean instilling habits (if you pause to go through something that should have been studied earlier, then you show that reading beforehand isn't really necessary).
- *People:* Who should be there (or not) and what roles individuals should have.
- *Environment:* A meeting will go much more smoothly if people attending are comfortable and if there are no interruptions (so organise the drinks first and switch phones onto silent before you start).

Then, at the appointed hour, you must take charge and make the meeting go well, making it clear to everyone that they must:

- Be prepared.
- Listen carefully.
- Make notes.
- Say what they think, keeping comments clear, succinct and to the point (while being sufficiently assertive to do so).
- Deal through the Chair and respect the agenda and any meeting formalities.
- Never resort to abuse, but be prepared to fight their corner on a rational business-like basis to make a point.
- Be open-minded and respect others' points of view (though not necessarily agreeing with them).

Politeness coupled with firmness, assertiveness rather than aggression – all these make for a good meeting.

Leading a meeting

Even a simple meeting needs someone in the chair. That does *not* imply that whoever that is should be the most senior person present, do most of the talking or even lead the talking, or that they should be formally called "Chairperson" – but someone must *direct* the meeting.

An effective Chair means:

- The meeting will better focus on its objectives.
- Discussion can be kept more constructive.
- A thorough review can be assured before what may otherwise be ad hoc decisions are taken.
- All sides of the argument or case can be reflected and balanced.
- Proceedings can be kept business-like and less argumentative (even when dealing with contentious issues).

A good chairperson will lead the meeting, handle the discussion and act to see objectives are met promptly, efficiently and effectively and without wasting time. Some of what must be done is simple, much is common sense; the whole of the role is important. Two simple but key rules that any chairperson can usefully deploy (and which others should respect) are:

1. Only one person may talk at a time.
2. The chairperson decides who (should this be necessary).

Already all this should begin to highlight the qualities of the person who will make a good chairperson. The following checklist of responsibilities provides more detail:

CHECKLIST: **The meeting leader's responsibilities**

Whoever is in the chair must:

- Be prepared (preferably more thoroughly than others attending).
- Set and keep to the agenda, keeping everyone and everything to time (an ability to start, stop and run on time throughout is especially impressive to others).

- Pre-organise and manage the environment (everything from visual aids to refreshments).
- Set the rules and keep control, yet encourage discussion, letting people have their say in an orderly way.
- Listen carefully and continuously and make any appropriate notes.
- Be able to field questions, arbitrate in debate and referee (and ultimately end) arguments.
- See, and deal with, both sides of any debate.
- Ask questions if clarification is necessary and summarise regularly, clearly and succinctly.
- Bring matters to a conclusion, prompt and record decisions and maintain a reasonable consensus (this may extend to attending to administrative matters after the meeting).

This list illustrates the range and nature of the tasks involved. It also shows clearly that there are skills involved (perhaps skills which might usefully be studied, learned and practised).

Finally: two further points are worth a word.

Getting off to a good start

The best meetings start well, continue well and end well. The Chair should begin a meeting in a way that:

- Is positive and business-like.
- Makes the purpose (and procedure) clear.
- Establishes their authority and right to be in charge.
- Creates the right atmosphere (whether to prompt creative thinking, say, or detailed analysis of figures).
- Generates interest and enthusiasm for the topics (yes, even if at a tedious regular review).

It usually helps if the Chair involves others early on, rather than beginning with a lengthy monologue.

Prompting discussion

You want contributions from everyone (or why are they present?). So, to ensure that subsequent decisions are made on all the appropriate facts and information you may (sometimes) need to prompt discussion:

- Watch for specific reasons for silence (someone fearing rejection, unprepared or simply needing encouragement). Ask for views and prompt open, considered comments.
- Questions must be unambiguous and you should use both open and closed questions (explained in the last chapter). Right?
- Do not lead with your own opinions. You are unlikely to encourage creative suggestions by highlighting your own thoughts first: *I think that's excellent, what do others think?*

Too often meetings are unproductive or unconstructive not because how they are undertaken is ill-considered, but because making them successful is hardly considered at all. There is a real opportunity here – maybe one worth convening a meeting to discuss?

ALMOST FACE-TO-FACE

Two other methods of communication deserve a mention and seem to fit here.

First, "conference systems". I put that in inverted commas as there are many systems (and given the ongoing technological revolution methods will doubtless continue to evolve). They can be useful, allowing two people, or a group of people, perhaps in widely separated locations to communicate as if in a meeting.

While in some ways these are just like any other communication, two things perhaps need care:

- In *voice only* interactions, implications mirror telephoning (see next heading) and allowance must be made for the lack of visual information. Voice alone must clearly express everything intended and no hand gestures or facial expressions can be involved. This should be borne in mind both as you communicate and as you listen; more clarification than usual may be necessary as visual signs of agreement or objection may not be visible or clear.
- *Discipline* is necessary with many voices at once making the exchange disjointed and often pointless. Contacts may need more planning and organisation: a hierarchy of contact may need agreement for group communication (when some sort of chairing role may help), and individual contributions need to be particularly succinct and to the point.

Secondly, a few points about **telephone contact**, some of which are also relevant to conference communication.

When the phone rings you may not know who it is calling, so the response must always assume that how you answer matters.

The basic rules include the need to:

- Answer **promptly.**
- **Identify** yourself (it may be sufficient to say your (full) name: *Patrick Forsyth,* or you may prefer something more, *Good morning, this is Patrick Forsyth* or need something that includes a departmental or functional description *(Good morning, Sales Office, Mary Bolton speaking)*. This may, in part, be a matter of policy and consistency around a department and should link neatly to whatever a switchboard will say.
- **Hold the phone properly**: Obvious perhaps, but it

really does impede hearing if the handset is tucked under the chin or pushed aside as you reach for something. You must be clearly audible.

- **Decide whether to take the call or not**: Some calls, say from customers, may always need to be taken immediately. But the telephone is obtrusive and, if you are busy, and a colleague simply wants a word it may be acceptable to delay it: *I'm just finishing an important report, may I call you in half an hour?* Alternatively, the call may need transferring – something that must always be explained and handled promptly.

- Adopt an **appropriate manner:** This is not a question of insincerity or acting, just that we want to emphasise certain traits more with some people than others – a nice friendly, but not over familiar, tone with customers, and so on.

- Once into the call, **speak clearly (and a fraction slower than normal)**, certainly do not gabble, and try to keep your thoughts organised. It is difficult talking instantly (because the phone has rung) and, as you cannot see the other person, thoughts can easily become jumbled as a result.

- It may help to **signpost**: to say something that tells the caller what is coming e.g. *Right, you want an update about the new brochure design project. Let me go through it, the key things are probably the costs, the copy, the design and the timing; now first costs....* This helps both parties, giving the caller the opportunity to amend the list and giving you a list to keep in mind (note down?) and work through.

- Always **listen carefully**: It may be a voice only medium, but it is two-way. Do not do all the talking, make it clear you are listening by acknowledging points as they go along and **make notes as necessary.**

- Be **polite**: Of course, there could just be times you *need* to shout at someone! (colleagues if not customers) More usually though it is important to maintain reasonable courtesies and, with voice only, it can be easy to sound, say, abrupt when you are simply trying to be prompt.

- Be aware of **pauses**. If you say, *Hold on a sec, I'll get the file,* remember the pause seems long to the person waiting. Sometimes it's better to suggest getting everything in front of you and phoning back. Or you can split what would otherwise seem a long pause into two shorter, pauses by saying something like, *Right, I've got the file, I'll just turn up the figures you want.*
- Have **the right information to hand**: Many calls are repetitive in nature and you can handle them more efficiently if you anticipate what information is needed and have it to hand (and in a form that is convenient to deal with on the phone e.g. papers in ring binders lie flat and don't need to be held open when you are already trying to hold the handset and write notes).
- Be **careful with names**: People are sensitive about their names. Get them right early on – ask for the spelling or how to pronounce them if necessary, and use them occasionally during the conversation. It is annoying as an outside caller if you are asked your name by the switchboard, a secretary and the person who handles the call and then, moments later, they ask: *What was your name again?*
- If **bad reception** should really hinder communication it may be better to call them back.
- Finally, **hang up last**: now you cannot both do this! But with something like a customer call, it's fine to be the first to initiate the end of the call or to say *goodbye* but if you put the phone down last it avoids the caller thinking of something else and feeling they have been left over hastily.

Doubtless such a list could be extended, but the above captures the essentials.

CHAPTER 4

PUTTING IT IN WRITING

*What is written without effort
is in general read without pleasure.*

Samuel Johnson

THE NATURE OF THE WRITTEN WORD

In a busy work life writing anything can be a chore. There are surely more important things to be done, people to meet, decisions to be made, action to be taken. Yet all of these things and more can be dependent on written communication. An email may set up a meeting, a report may present a case and prompt a decision, and a proposal may act persuasively to make sure certain action is taken or a particular option is selected.

But reading business papers can be a chore also, and they will not achieve their purpose unless they are read, understood and do their job well enough to actively prompt the reader to action.

Business writing must *earn* a reading.

Consider writing with your reader's hat on for a moment. Do you read everything that crosses your desk? Do you read every word of the things you do read? Do you read everything from the first word through in sequence, or do you dip into things? Almost certainly the answers make it clear that not all writing is treated equally. Some documents are more likely to be read than others. Of course, some subjects demand your attention. For instance, who ignores a personal note from the Managing Director? But the fact that some things have to be read does not make their reading any easier or more pleasurable.

Good writing, which means, not least, something that is easy to read and understand, will always be likely to get more attention than sloppy writing. Yet we all know that prevailing standards in this area are by no means universally good.

Why is this? Maybe it is education, or lack of it. Often school assists little with the kind of writing we find ourselves having to do once we are in the workplace. Maybe it is lack of feedback; perhaps managers are too tolerant of what is put in front of them. If more of it was rejected, and had to be rewritten, then more attention might be brought to bear on the task.

Habits are important here too. We all develop a style of writing and may find it difficult to shift away from it. Worse, bad habits may be reinforced by practice. For example, the ubiquitous standard online document can often be used year after year with no one prepared to say: *Scrap it*, even if they notice how inadequate it is.

A fragile process

We can all recognise the really bad report, without structure or style, but with an excess of jargon, convoluted sentences and which prompts the thought: *What is it trying to say*? But such documents do not have to be a complete mess to fail in their purpose. They are inherently fragile. One wrongly chosen word may dilute understanding or act to remove what would otherwise make a positive impression .

Even something as simple as a spelling mistake (and, no, computer spell checkers are not infallible) may have a negative effect; I once saw work lost by a consultant who spelt the name of a company as diary rather than dairy. As a very first rule to drum into your subconscious – check, check and check again. Whether the cause of a document being worse than it should be is major or minor, the damage is the same; the quality of writing matters.

A major opportunity

Whatever the reasons for poor writing may be, suffice to say that, if prevailing standards are low, then there is a major opportunity here for those who better that standard. More so for those who excel. Bad documents might just come back to haunt you later.

So, business writing is a vital skill. There may be a great deal hanging on a document doing the job it is intended to do – a decision, a sale, a financial result, or a personal reputation. For those who can acquire sound skills in this area very real opportunities exist. The more you have to write, and the more important the documents you create, then the truer this is. Quite simply, if you write well then you are more likely to achieve your business goals.

This point cannot be overemphasised. One sheet of paper may not change the world, but – well written – it can influence many events in a way that affects results and those doing the writing.

And you can write well. We may not all aspire to or succeed in writing the great novel, but most people can learn to turn out good business writing – writing that is well tailored to its purpose and likely to create the effect it intends. This chapter reviews some of the approaches that can make business writing easier, quicker (a worthwhile end in itself) and, most importantly, that makes documents more likely to achieve their purpose.

Good business writing need not be difficult. It is a skill, which can be developed with study and practice. Some effort may be involved, and certainly practice helps, but it could be worse. Somerset Maugham is quoted as saying:

There are three rules for writing the novel. Unfortunately, no one knows what they are.

Business writing is not so dependent on creativity, though this is involved, but it *is* subject to certain rules. Rules, of course, are made to be broken. But they do act as useful guidelines and can therefore be a help. Here we review how to go about the writing task and, in part, when to follow the rules and when to break them.

WHAT MAKES GOOD BUSINESS WRITING?

However a case is presented, even if there is no paper, as with something sent through email for example, it has to be written. Email, incidentally, is dealt with separately in Chapter 5.

With even brief communications prone to misunderstanding, how much more potential for misunderstanding does a twenty-five page report present? And with written communication the danger is that any confusion lasts. There is not necessarily an immediate opportunity to check (the writer might be a hundred miles away), and a misunderstanding on page 3 may skew the whole message taken from an entire report.

Serious, and very serious

Once something is in writing any error that causes misunderstanding is made permanent, at least for a while. The dangers of ill-thought out writing vary:
- *It may be wrong*, but still manage to convey its meaning. For instance: the hotel notice quoted earlier saying: *In the interest of security, please ensure that your bedroom door is fully closed when entering or*

leaving your room. It may amuse – and be a good trick if you can do it – but it will probably be understood. No great harm done perhaps, though in a service business any fault tends to highlight the possibility of other, more serious, faults.

- *It may try too hard to please*, ending up giving the wrong impression. In one Renaissance Hotel there are signs on the coffee shop tables that say: *COURTESY OF CHOICE: The concept and symbol of "Courtesy of Choice" reflects the centuries-old philosophy that acknowledges differences while allowing them to exist together in harmony. "Courtesy of Choice" accommodates the preferences of individuals by offering both smoking and non-smoking areas in the spirit of conviviality and mutual respect.* An absurd over politeness just ends up making the message sound rude – this restaurant has both smoking and non-smoking areas and if you find yourself next to a smoker, tough. It does matter.

- *It may be incomprehensible.* A press release is an important piece of writing. One, quoted in the national press, was sent out by the consulting group Accenture. The item commented that Accenture envisioned: *A world where economic activity is ubiquitous, unbounded by the traditional definitions of commerce and universal.* Er, yes – or rather, no. The newspaper referred not to the content of the release, only to the fact that it contained a statement so wholly gobbledegook as to have no meaning at all. It is sad when the writing is so bad that it achieves less than nothing.

You could doubtless extend such a list of examples extensively. The point here is clear: it is all too easy for the written word to fail. Such things were probably the subject of some thought and checking, but not enough. Put pen to paper, as it were, and you step onto dangerous ground. So, the first requirement of good business writing is *clarity*. A good report needs thinking about if it is to be clear, and it should never be taken for granted that understanding will be automatically generated by what we write. As was said earlier, you may want to recall the chapter on preparation.

It is more likely that we will give due consideration to clarity, and give the attention it needs to achieving it, if we are clear about the purpose of any report we may write.

WHY ARE WE WRITING?

Exactly why anything is written is important. This may seem self-evident, yet many reports, for instance, are no more than something "about" their topic. Their purpose is not clear. Without clear intentions the tendency is for the report to ramble, to go round and round and not come to any clear conclusion.

Documents may be written for many reasons, for example they may intend to inform, motivate or persuade – any of the intentions listed earlier – and often more than one intention is aimed at and different messages or emphasis for different people adds further complexity.

Reader expectations

If a document is to be well received, then it must meet certain expectations of its readers. Before going into these let us consider generally what conditions such expectations. Psychologists talk about what they call "cognitive cost". This is best explained by example. Imagine you want to do something that is other than routine with some electronic gadget, so you get out the instruction book. Big mistake. You open it and the two-page spread shouts at you: *This is going to be difficult*! Such a document has what is called a high *cognitive cost* – rather than appearing inviting, even a cursory look is off-putting.

People are wary of this effect. They look at any document almost *expecting* reading it to be hard work. If they discover it looks easier and more inviting than they thought (a low cognitive cost), then they are likely to read it with more enthusiasm. What gives people the feeling, both at first glance and as they get further into it, that a document is not to be avoided on principle? In no particular order, the following are some of the key factors readers like:

- *Brief*: Obviously something shorter is likely to appear to be easier to read than something long, but what really matters is that a report is of an appropriate length for its topic and purpose. Perhaps the best word to apply is *succinct* – to the point, long enough to say what is necessary and no more. A report may be 10 pages long, or 50, and still qualify for this description.
- *Succinct:* This makes clear that length is inextricably linked to message. If there is a rule, then it is to make something long enough to carry the message, then stop.
- *Relevant*: This goes with the first point. Not overlong, covering what is required, and without irrelevant content or digression. *Note:* Comprehensiveness is *never* an objective. If a report, say, touched on absolutely everything then it would certainly be too long. In fact, you always have to be selective; if you do not say everything, then everything you do say is a choice – you need to make good content choices.
- *Clear*: People must be able to understand it. And this applies in a number of ways, for example, it should be clearly written (in the sense of not being convoluted), and use appropriate language – no intended reader should have to look up every second word in a dictionary.
- *Precise*: Saying exactly what is necessary and not constantly digressing without purpose.

- *In "our language"*: In other words, using a level and style of language that is likely to make sense to the target reader, and which displays evidence of being designed to do so.
- *Simple*: Avoiding unnecessary complexity.
- *Well-structured:* so that it proceeds logically through a sequence that is clear and makes sense as a sensible way of dealing with the message.
- *Descriptive*: Of which more anon; here suffice to say that if there is a need to paint a picture it must do so in a way that gets that picture over.

All these have in common that they can act to make reading easier. Further, they act cumulatively, that is the more things are right in each of these ways, the clearer the writing will be. If the impression is given that attention has *actively* been given to making the reader's task easier, so much the better.

Such factors are worth personalising to the kind of people to whom you must write. Whether this is internal, colleagues perhaps, or external, for instance customers or collaborators, you need to be clear what your communications have to do and what kind of expectations exist at the other end. For example, a technical person may have different expectations from a layman and may be looking to check a level of detail that must exist and be clearly expressed for the report to be acceptable to them.

The reader's perspective

It follows logically from what has been said in this chapter so far that good business writing must reflect the needs of the reader. Such writing cannot be undertaken in a vacuum. It is not simply an opportunity for the writer to say things as they want. Ultimately only readers can judge a document to be good. Thus their perspective is the starting point and as the writer you need to think about who the intended readers are, how they think, how they view the topic of the report, what their experience to date is of the issues, and how they are likely to react to what you have to say. This links to preparation, which was dealt with in depth earlier.

Powerful habits

Habit, and the ongoing pressure of business, can combine to push people into writing on "automatic pilot". Sometimes, if you critique something that you wrote, or that went out from your department, you can clearly see something that is wrong. A sentence does not make sense, a point fails to get across or a description confuses rather than clarifies. Usually the reason this has occurred is not that the writer really thought this was the best sentence or phrase and got it wrong. Rather it was because there was inadequate thought, or none at all.

Habits can be difficult to break and the end result can be a plethora of material moving around organisations couched in a kind of gobbledegook or what some call "office-speak".

Earning a reading

The moral here is clear. Good writing does not just happen. It needs some thought and some effort (and some study, with which we aim to assist). The process needs to be actively worked at if the result is going to do the job you have in mind, and do it with some certainty.

Good habits are as powerful as bad. A shift from one to another is possible and the rewards in this case make the game very much worth the candle. Think what good writing skills can achieve.

The rewards of excellence

Consider the example of reports; they can influence action. But they also act to create an image of the writer. All the different ways in which people interrelate and act together, cumulatively and progressively, build up and maintain an image of each individual. Some ways may play a disproportionate part, and report writing is one such. There are two reasons why this effect is important:

- Reports, unlike more transient means of communication, can last. They are passed around, considered and remain on the record; more so if they are about important issues.
- Because not everyone can write a good report, people can be impressed by a clear ability to marshal an argument and put it over in writing.

As a result, reports represent an opportunity, or in fact two opportunities. Reports – at least, good ones – can be instrumental in prompting action; hopefully action that you want. They are also important to your profile. They say something about the kind of person you are and how you are to work with. In a sense there are situations where you want to make sure certain personal qualities shine through. A case may be supported by it being clear that it is presented by someone who gives attention to details, for instance.

Longer-term, the view taken of someone by their management may be influenced by their regularly reading what they regard as good reports. So, next time you are burning the midnight oil to get some seemingly tedious report (or any other document for that matter) finalised, think of it as the business equivalent of an open goal and, remember, it could literally be affecting your chances of promotion!

A significant opportunity

Reports demand detailed work. Their preparation may, on occasion, seem tedious. They certainly need adequate time set aside for them. But as the old saying has it: if a job is worth doing, it is worth doing well. It may take no more time to prepare a good report than it does to prepare a lacklustre one; so too for any document.

If whatever you write is clear, focused and set out so as to earn a reading, then you are more likely to achieve your purpose and to enhance your profile as the writer. Both these results are surely worthwhile. But the job still has to be done, the words still have to be written, and faced with a blank sheet or screen this can be a daunting task (writing a book of this length certainly qualifies me to say that!). Go about it in the right way however and it does become possible.

By using reports as an example, I do not want to exclude other written documents and with all such written work remember that:

- Communication has inherent dangers, clear communication needs to be well-considered.
- Documents will only achieve their purpose if the writer is clear in their mind what they are seeking to achieve.
- Readers are more important than the writer; write for others not for yourself.
- You must beware of old habits and work to establish good ones.
- Documents are potentially powerful tools – powerful in action terms, and powerful in contributing to personal profiles.

The writing process: what to say and how to say it

If you undertake to engender a totality of meaning that corresponds with the cognition of others seeking to intake a communication from the content you display in your writing there is a greater likelihood of subsequent action being that which you desire.

You are correct. That is not a good start. If I want to say:

if you write well, people will understand and be more likely to react as you wish then I should say just that. But it makes a good point with which to start this section. Language, and how you use it, matters. Exactly how you put things has a direct bearing on how they are received; and that in turn has a direct bearing on how well you succeed in your objectives.

It is clear language that makes a difference. But this is a serious understatement; language can make a very considerable difference. And it can make a difference in many different ways, as I will illustrate.

How you *need* to write must stem as much as anything from the view your intended readers have of what they want to read; or indeed are prepared to read. Consider four broad elements first. Readers want documents to be understandable, readable, straightforward and natural.

Understandable

Clarity has been mentioned already. Its necessity may seem to go without saying, though some, at least, of what one sees of prevailing standards suggests the opposite. It is all too easy to find everyday examples of wording that is less than clear. A favourite is a sign you still see in some shops: *EARS PIERCED, WHILE YOU WAIT*. There is some other way? Maybe there has been a new technological development.

Clarity is assisted by many of the elements mentioned here, but three factors help immensely:

- *Using the right words*: For example, are you writing about *recommendations* or *options*, about *objectives* (desired results) or *strategies* (routes to achieving objectives), and when do you use *aims* or *goals?*
- *Using the right phrases*: What is *24-hour service* exactly, other than not sufficiently specific. Ditto *personal service*? Is this just saying something is done by people? If so it is hardly a glimpse of

anything but the obvious; perhaps it needs expanding to explain the nature, and perhaps excellence, of a particular service approach
- *Selecting and arranging words* to ensure your meaning is clear: for example, saying, *At this stage, the arrangement is...* implies that later it will be something else, when this might not be intended. Saying, *After working late into the night, the report will be with you this afternoon*, seems to imply (because of the sequence and arrangement of words) that it is the report that was working late.

Even changing a word or two can make a difference. Saying something is *quite nice* is so bland that, if applied to something that is *hugely enjoyable* the understatement is almost insulting. The emphasis may be inadequate, but at least the word *nice* makes it clear that something positive is being said. Blandness is certainly to be avoided as it is unlikely to add power to your message. Choosing the wrong word is another matter – that might confuse, upset – or worse. The following examples of word use are designed to illustrate the danger:

- *Continuous* (unbroken or uninterrupted); *Continual* (repeated or recurring) – a project might be continuous (in process all the time), but work on it is more likely to be continual (unless you never sleep).
- Are you *uninterested* in a proposal or *disinterested* in it? The first implies you are apathetic and care not either way, the latter means you have nothing to gain from it.
- Similarly *dissatisfied* and *unsatisfied* should not be confused. Disappointed or needing more of something respectively.
- You might want to do something *expeditious* (quick and efficient), but saying it is *expedient* might not be

so well regarded as it means only that something is convenient (not always a good reason to do anything).
- *Fortuitous* implies something happening accidentally; it does not mean fortunate.
- If you are a *practical* person then you are effective, if something is *practicable* it is merely possible to do, and *pragmatic* is something meant to be effective (rather than proven to be).

One wrong word may do damage. What's more, particularly when closely associated, it can quickly create nonsense: *This practicable approach will ensure the practicable project will be continuous, it is fortuitous that I am uninterested in it and I am sure I will not be unsatisfied to see it start*.

Inaccurate use of language will not help you put a message over well even if it only annoys rather than confuses, e.g. writing *12 noon* when *noon* tells you everything you need to know, or talking about an *ATM machine* when the M stands for machine (a machine machine?). Some care, maybe even some checking or study, may be useful.

Readable

Readability is difficult to define, but we all know it when we experience it. Your writing must flow. One point must lead to another and the writing must strike the right tone; inject a little variety and, above all, there must be a logical, and visible, structure to carry the message along. The technique mentioned of "signposting" – briefly flagging what is to come – helps in a practical sense to get the reader understanding where something is going. It makes them read on, content that the direction is sensible (this section starts just that way, listing points to come, of which "readable" is the second). It is difficult to overuse signposting and it can be utilised at several levels within a text.

Straightforward

This means simply put. Follow the well-known acronym KISS - Keep It Simple, Stupid. Thus use:

- *Short words*: Why *elucidate* something when you can *explain*? Why *reimbursements* rather than *expenses?* Similarly, although *experiment* and *test* do have slightly different meanings, in a general sense *test* may be better; or you could use *try*.
- *Short phrases*: Do not say *at this moment in time* when you mean *now*, or *respectfully acknowledge* something, a suggestion perhaps, when you can simply say *thank you*.
- *Short sentences*: Having too many overlong sentences is a frequent characteristic of business reports. Short ones are good. However, they should be mixed in with longer ones, or reading becomes rather like the action of a machine gun. Many reports contain sentences that are overlong, often because they mix two rather different points. Break these into two and the overall readability improves.
- *Short paragraphs*: If there are plenty of headings and bullet points it may be difficult to get this wrong, but keep an eye on it. Regular and appropriate breaks as the message builds up, particularly if reading on-screen, do make for easier reading.

Natural

In the same way that some people are said, disparagingly, to have a "telephone voice", so some write in an unnatural fashion. Such a style may just be old fashioned or bureaucratic. However, it could be made worse by attempts to create self-importance, or to make a topic seem weightier than it is. Just a few words can change the tone: saying *the writer* may easily sound pompous, for instance, especially if there is no reason not to say *I (or me)*.

The moral here is clear and provides a guideline for good writing. Business documents do need some formality, but they are, after all, an alternative to talking to people. They should be as close to speech as is reasonably possible. It is not suggested that you overdo this, either by becoming too chatty or by writing, say, *won't* (which you might acceptably say), when *will not* is generally more suitable. However, if you compose what you write much as you would say it and then tighten it up, the end result is often better than when you set out to create something that is "formal business writing".

The four factors above have wide influence on writing style, but they do not act alone. Other points are important, and link to reader expectations. Writing needs to be based very much on what people say they want in what they read. As was said earlier, this means: brief, succinct, relevant, precise, clear, and in "our" language.

Readers' dislikes

Readers also have hopes that what they must read will *not* be:

- *Introspective:* It is appropriate in most business documents to use the word *you* more than *I* (or *we, the company, the department* etc.). Thus saying: *I will circulate more detailed information soon* might be better phrased as: *You will receive more information (from me) soon*. More so, perhaps, if you add a phrase like: *So that you can judge for yourselves*. This approach is especially important if there is persuasion involved.
- *Talking down: As an expert, I can tell you this must be avoided, you must never...* Bad start – it sounds condescending. You are only likely to carry people with you if you avoid this kind of thing. As a

schools broadcast on radio put it: *Never talk down to people, never be condescending. You do know what condescending means don't you?* Enough said.

- *Biased*: At least where it intends not to be. A manager writing something to staff setting out why they think something is a good idea, and then asking for their staff's views, may prompt more agreement than is actually felt.

- *Politically incorrect*: There is considerable sensitivity about this these days that should neither be ignored nor underestimated. As there is still no word that means "he or she", some contrivance may occasionally be necessary in this respect. Similarly, choice of words needs care. Sometimes such things might seem somewhat silly. But if it matters, it matters, and while the way you write should not become awkward or contrived to accommodate these issues, some care is necessary.

There is a considerable amount to bear in mind here and the focus must be on the reader throughout. However, you must not forget your own position as the writer and there are things here also that must be incorporated into the way you write.

The writer's approach

Every organisation has an image. The only question is whether this just happens, for good or ill, or if it is seen as something to actively create, maintain and make positive. Similarly, every report or proposal you write says something about you, whether you like it or not. And it matters. The profile wittingly or unwittingly presented may influence whether people believe, trust or like you. It may influence how they feel about your expertise, or whether they can see themselves agreeing with you or doing business with you.

Your personal profile is not only an influence in your job, one that links to the objectives you have, it also potentially affects your career. Surely it is unavoidable that, given the profusion of paperwork in most organisations, what you write progressively typecasts you in the eyes of others – including your boss – as the sort of person who is going places, or not.

It bears thinking about.

Certainly your prevailing style, and what a particular document says about you, is worth thinking about. If there is an inevitable subtext of this sort, you cannot afford to let it go by default, you need to consciously influence it. Start by considering what you want people to think of you. Take a simple point. You want to be thought of as efficient. Then the style of the document surely says something about this. If it is good, contains everything the reader wants, and certainly if it covers everything it said it would, then a sense of efficiency surely follows.

The same applies to many characteristics: being seen as knowledgeable, experienced, authoritative and so on. As has been said all such characteristics are worth considering to ascertain exactly how you achieve the effect you want. Such images are cumulative. They build up over time and can assist in the establishment and maintenance of relationships. Whether this is with a colleague, a customer, or concerned with establishing with the boss that you are a good person to work with (as well as good at your work), the influence can be powerful.

Similarly, you might have in mind a list of characteristics you actively want to avoid seeming to embrace. For example appearing: dogmatic, patronising, inflexible, old fashioned, or whatever, in your job, might do you little good. Some other characteristics are sometimes to be emphasised, sometimes not. Stubbornness is perhaps a good example.

Such images are not created in a word. There is more to

appearing honest than writing: *Let me be completely honest* (which might actually ring alarm bells!). Your intended profile will come, in part, from specifics such as choice of words, but also from the whole way in which you use language. So there's more about language to consider.

The use of language

How language is used makes a difference to exactly how a message is received. The importance of using the right word has already been touched on, but the kind of difference we are talking about can be well demonstrated by changing no more than one word. For example, consider the first sentence after the last heading: *How language is used makes a difference to exactly how a message is received*. Add one word: ... *makes a big difference to...*

Now let us see what changing that word "big" does: it is surely a little different to say: .... *makes a great difference...* and there are many alternatives, all with varying meaning: *real, powerful, considerable, vast, special, large, important.* And more. In context of what I am actually saying here, powerful is a good word. It is not just a question of how you use language, but what you achieve by your use of it.

Note: No business writer should be without access to both a dictionary and thesaurus; the latter is often the most useful.

Making language work for you

Often business writing is almost wholly without adjectives. Yet surely one of the first purposes of language is to be *descriptive*. Most writing necessitates the need to paint a picture to some degree at least. Contrast two phrases: *Smooth as silk* and *Sort of shiny*.

The first (used as a slogan by Thai Airways) conjures up

a clear and precise picture, or certainly does for anyone who has seen and touched silk. The second might mean almost anything; dead wet fish are sort of shiny, but they are hardly to be compared with the touch of silk. Further, an even more descriptive phrase may be required; what about *slippery as a freshly buttered ice-rink*. Could anyone think this meant other than *really, really* slippery?

The question of expectation of complexity (and cognitive cost) was mentioned earlier, and to some extent it does not matter whether something is short or long; if it just makes things effortlessly clear, it is appreciated. And if it is both descriptive and makes something easier to understand then readers are doubly appreciative.

Clear description may need working at, but the effort is worthwhile. Trainers often ask a meeting venue to set up for a seminar arranging a group *in a U shape*. You can put people in a U around a boardroom-style table. But more often it means a U in the sense of an open U, one that gives the trainer the ability to stand within the U to work with delegates. Two different layouts, which both demand precise description.

Description is important, but sometimes we want more than that. We may want an element of something being descriptive, and also **memorable.** This is achieved in two ways: first by something that is descriptive yet unusual, secondly, when it is descriptive and unexpected.

Returning to the venue theme above, a conference executive describing, as part of an explanation about room layouts, a U shape as being one that: *puts everyone in the front row* is being descriptive and memorable because, while clear, it is also an unusual way of expressing it. Such phrases work well and are worth searching for.

As an example of the second route to being memorable, consider a description I once put in a report. In summarising a Perception Survey (researching the views customers and contacts held of a client organisation) I wanted to describe how the majority of people reported. They liked them, were well-disposed towards using them, but also found them a little bureaucratic, slow and less efficient and innovative than they would ideally like. I wrote that they were seen as

...being like a comfortable, but threadbare old sofa, when people wanted them to be like a modern, leather executive chair.

This is clearly descriptive, but it gained from being not just unusual, but by being really not the kind of phrase typically used in business writing. Its being memorable was confirmed, because it rang bells and at subsequent meetings was used by the organisation's own people to describe the changes that the study had highlighted as necessary.

There are occasions where this kind of approach works well, not least in ensuring something about the writer is expressed along the way. Some phrases or passages may draw strength because the reader would never feel it was quite appropriate to put it like that themselves, yet find they like reading it.

Another aspect you may want, on occasion, to put into your writing is **emotion**. If you want to seem enthusiastic, interested, surprised – whatever – this must show. A dead, passive style: *.... the results were not quite as expected, they showed that....* is not the same as one that characterises what is said with emotion: *You will be surprised by the results, which showed that...* Both may be appropriate in context and there might be occasion to strengthen it further: T*the results will amaze.*

Consider this: how often when you are searching for the right phrase do you reject something as either not sufficiently formal (or conventional)? Be honest. Many are on the brink of putting down something that will be memorable or powerful, then play safe and opt for something else. It may be adequate, but can fail to impress and end up being a lost opportunity.

Mistakes to avoid

Some things may act to dilute the power of your writing. They may or may not be technically wrong, but they end up reducing your effectiveness and making your objectives less certain to be achieved.

Blandness

Watch out! This is a regular trap for the business writer. It happens not so much because you *choose* the wrong thing to write, but because you are writing on automatic pilot *without* thought, or at least not much thought, and make no real conscious choice.

What does it mean to say something is:

- *Quite* good (or bad)? or:
- *Rather* expensive?
- Making *very slow* progress?

What exactly is:

- An *attractive* promotion? (As opposed to a profit generating one, perhaps).
- A *slight* delay? (For a moment or a month?).

All these give only a vague impression. Ask yourself exactly what you want to express, then choose language that does just that.

"Office speak"

This is another all too common component of some business writing, much of it passed on from one person to another without comment or change. It may confuse little, but adds little either, other than an old fashioned feel.

Phrases such as:

- Enclosed *for your perusal* (even *enclosed for your interest* may be unsuitable. You may need to tell them why it should be of interest, or *enclosed* alone may suffice).
- *We respectfully acknowledge receipt of* (why not say: *Thank you for…*?).
- *In the event that* (*if*, is surely better).
- *Very high speed operation* (*fast*, or state just how fast).

Avoid such trite approaches like the plague (sic), and work to change the habit of any "pet" phrases you use all too easily, all too often and inappropriately.

Language of "fashion"

Language is changing all the time. New words and phrases enter the language almost daily, and are often linked to the use of technology. It is worth watching for the life cycle of such words because if you are out of step then they may fail to do the job you want. I notice three stages:

1. When it is too early to use them. When they will either not be understood, or seem silly or even like a failed attempt at trendiness.
2. When they work well.
3. When their use begins to date and sound wrong or inadequate.

Examples may date too, but let me try. When BBC Radio 4 talks about an "*upcoming*" event, then for some people, this is in its early stage and does not sound right at all; *forthcoming* will suit me well for a while longer.

On the other hand, what did we say before we said *mission statement*? This is certainly a term in current use. Most people in business appreciate its meaning and some have made good use of the thinking that goes into producing one.

What about a word or phrase that is past its best? To

suggest a common one: *user friendly*. When first used it was new, nicely descriptive and quickly began to be useful. Now with no single gadget on the entire planet not so described by its makers, it is becoming very weak.

Mistakes people hate

Some errors are actually well known to most people, yet they still slip through and there is a category that simply shares the fact that many people find them annoying when they are on the receiving end. A simple example is the word *unique*, which is so often used with an adjective. Unique means something is like nothing else. Nothing can be *very unique* or *greatly unique*, even the company whose brochure I saw with the words *very unique* occurring three times in one paragraph, do not in fact have a product that is more than just unique even once. Think of similar examples that annoy you and avoid them too.

Others here include the likes of:
- *Different to* (different from).
- *Less,* which relates to quantity, when numbers (where fewer would be correct) are involved.

Another area for care is with unnecessary apostrophe's (sic), which are becoming a modern plague.

Clichés

This is a somewhat difficult one. Any overused phrase can become categorised as a cliché. Yet a phrase like *putting the cart before the horse* is not only well known but establishes an instant and precise vision and can therefore be useful. In a sense people like to conjure up a familiar image and so such phrases should not always be avoided, and business may not be the place for creative alternatives like *spread the butter before the jam*.

Following the rules

What about **grammar, syntax** and **punctuation**? Of course they matter along with typos. Spellcheckers pick up many errors these days though you need to cheque (sic) carefully as they will not highlight all.

Certain things can jar. For example:

- *Poor punctuation*: Too little is exhausting to read, especially coupled with long sentences. Too much becomes affected seeming and awkward. Certain rules do matter here, but the simplest guide is probably breathing. We learn to punctuate speech long before we write anything, so in writing all that is really necessary is a conscious inclusion of the pauses. The length of pause and the nature of what is being said indicates the likely solution. In some ways better too much than not enough.

- *Tautology* (unnecessary repetition) of which the classic example is people who say, *I, myself personally* is to be avoided. Do not *export overseas,* simply export, do not indulge in *forward planning,* simply plan.

- *Oxymorons* (word combinations that are contradictory) may sound silly – *distinctly foggy* – or be current good ways of expressing something – *deafening silence*. Some sentences can cause similar problems of contradiction: *I never make predictions and I never will*.

Other things are still regarded as rules by purists but work well in business writing and are now in current use. A good example here is the rule stating that you should never begin a sentence with the words "and" or "but". But you can. And it helps produce tighter writing and avoid overlong sentences. But... or rather however, it also makes another point; do not overuse this sort of thing.

Another similar rule is that sentences cannot be ended with

prepositions. Yet *He is a person worth talking to* really does sound easier on the ear than: *....with whom it is worth talking*. Winston Churchill is said to have responded to criticism about this with the famous line:

This is a type of arrant pedantry up with which I will not put.

Still, other rules may be broken only occasionally. Many of us have been taught never to split infinitives, and it thus comes under the annoyance category most of the time. There are exceptions however: would the most famous one in the world – Star Trek's *to boldly go where no man has gone before* – really be better as *to go boldly?* I don't think so.

Personal style

Finally, most people have, or develop, a way of writing that includes things they simply like. Why not indeed? For example, although rule books now say they are simply alternatives, I think that to say: *First, secondly... and thirdly...*, has much more elegance than beginning: *Firstly...* The reason why matters less than achieving an effect you feel is right.

It would be a duller world if we all did everything the same way and writing is no exception. There is no harm in using some things for no better reason than that you like them. It is likely to add variety to your writing, and make it seem distinctively different from that of other people, which may itself be useful.

Certainly, you should always be happy that what you write *sounds* right. So, to quote Keith Waterhouse:

If, after all this advice, a sentence still reads awkwardly, then what you have there is an awkward sentence. Demolish it and start again.

Summary

Overall, remember to:

- Make sure what you write is not only readable, but is designed for its readers.
- Put clarity first; understanding is the foundation of good business writing.
- Influence the subtext that provides an image of you, and ensure it works as you want.
- Make language work for you; be descriptive, be memorable.
- Make your writing correct, but make it individual.

Note: A broader treatment of this topic is available in my book *Business Writing* (also in the Smart Skills series).

CHAPTER 5

MAKING IT ELECTRONIC

The goal of computer science is to build something that will last until you've finished building it.

Douglas Adams

Some readers will remember sending faxes (or even telegrams way back). Recently, the range of means of communicating has grown beyond recognition and continues to evolve. Email is now ubiquitous and the most common form of daily communication. We also have the likes of Skype, Facebook, Instagram, Twitter, WebEx and many more.

Undoubtedly the mix will change and be added to and anything I say regarding a particular methodology may date quickly.

SOME FUNDAMENTAL FACTORS

However, there are principles here that are well-nigh perennial, so I will major on those and start with some factors that have a bearing across the range before commenting in more detail about email.

Choose your method

At the time of writing President Trump is becoming perhaps the most famous or infamous user of Twitter though one problem (among many?) is that it shows that it is very difficult to say anything worthwhile about any serious issue in a mere 280 characters; indeed some people find it difficult even to say anything intelligible at all.

Perhaps no further example is necessary to make the point that care is necessary in choosing the appropriate method with which to communicate. Sometimes methods go together in the way that a report may be summarised or explained in a formal presentation. Always the method must be chosen to ensure that the message is transferred successfully rather than just to be convenient to the sender.

That said, methods change, not least because of technology, and so too does the way in which they are viewed. Some things, like firing someone or, conversely, congratulating them are perhaps best not done by text message. A thank you letter is still appreciated and seen as special, but maybe only just, and I choose this example to show how perceptions change over time.

For some communications the electronic route is hampered by its essentially fragile nature. It can, after all, be deleted in a split second.

The dangers of brevity

Twitter is really short, but so too are texts and many an email. It has been said that the most common topic of emails is clarification – writing back to someone saying that that you are not quite sure what they meant. Brevity can be a virtue, but it very easily clashes with clarity. The quotation: *If I had more time, I would have written a shorter letter* is attributed to many people including Mark Twain. It makes a good point. It may seem easy to dash off a few words quickly, but achieving clarity may well need more thought.

The moral here is clear: be sure that what you write is absolutely clear and, if it's not, and making your message clear needs a few more words, then so be it. Nowhere is this truer than email and other things are worth thinking about too. For instance, how many people finding a website not entirely clear will make contact to clarify matters? They are more likely to go elsewhere. Websites usually contain a large amount of text, which must be clear and systems must be in place to ensure the information they present is kept up-to-date.

Note: Too many abbreviations, "text-speak" and the like, are an additional hazard where unthinking use can dilute understanding. Social habits may flow over into your work activities, but you need to think carefully about what is suitable, and clear, in a corporate context. Informality is fine – as long as it is considered and appropriate.

All this links firmly to the next point.

The dangers of poor checking

There seems to be something about much electronic messaging that means they are less checked than something more formal; certainly this is true of email. Partly this is haste, and so much seems to be treated as urgent these days. But it is also prompted by lack of thinking and bad habits.

Remember the job is not only to achieve understanding but also to project the right image and profile, something that may matter very much if you are writing to a customer or your boss. So any message needs to be right: well worded, punctuated and grammatical – all things that are there to help achieve clarity and thus achieve objectives.

So the moral is simple. First, resist sending something off without thinking about it – the instant reply to an email for instance. Secondly, check, check and check again. Even a misplaced comma can change the meaning: for example what will a comma do to this sentence: *Twelve months before he had taken up his new appointment?*

The dangers of inappropriate use

All sorts of social media, and email too, are easily (and regularly) misused. The least of the hazards is simply time-wasting; the internet is very moreish and much time is wasted on it. Productivity suffers and organisational rules may be broken.

More serious wrong use may range from ill-judged intended humour to more serious things including bullying or harassment. A little more is said about this in the context of email so here let me say simply: think before you act and avoid *anything and everything* that might fall into this category. The consequences of getting it wrong can be difficult, time-consuming and expensive, and can affect you, your organisation, reputations and even your job. You have been warned.

THE UBIQUITOUS EMAIL

The attractiveness of emailing is without doubt its speed. Mail is sent immediately when you click the 'Send' button. The speed of any reply is then dependent only on how regularly someone checks their email inbox and takes time to reply. As well as the risks attached, the fast to and fro nature of email communication can be positive – prompting rapid action and boosting efficiency.

Email versus snail mail

Email is usually less formal than writing a letter. But let me say this firmly and up front: the level of formality must be selected wisely.

There are those to whom you may write very informally (incorporating as many abbreviations, grammatical shortcuts, minimal punctuation and bizarre spellings as you wish) *as long as your meaning is clear*. But others (customers, senior colleagues) may resent this or think worse of you for it. Sometimes (often? usually?) an email must be as well-written as any important letter. It is safest to adopt a fairly formal style, certainly a clear one, and to err on the side of more rather than less formality if you are unsure. Proofreading and spell-checking is as important here as with many other documents.

The main purpose of email is not for lengthy communications but usually for short, direct information giving or gathering. Lengthy emails are difficult to read and absorb on screen. For this and other reasons, alternative means of communication are sometimes better selected (or an email may sometimes have a hard copy sent on). Longer information can be added as a document attached to an email, but you need to have confidence that someone will take time to read and see it as sufficiently important to do so.

Never forget just how easy it is to ignore an email. One click and it is gone in a spilt second and forever.

Disadvantages of email

Email is not universally wonderful. For instance:

- It is obviously impossible to communicate with someone electronically if the recipient is not online with access to their computer, phone or tablet.
- Email agreement can be just as legally binding as a formal document and treating it otherwise can cause problems.
- If technical problems put your system out of action this can cause problems and a back-up needs to be in place (it is not a question of if it happens, but when).
- Most junk email – or "spam" – is just as irritating as the junk mail that arrives through the letterbox. The

responsibility rests with the user and it is sensible to reduce its volume by having, and keeping up to date, software that filters it (though some always seems to slip through).

- Caution should be exercised in opening emails and attachments from unknown recipients as viruses, Trojan horses and worms can invade the computer system if care is not taken; more of this later.

Already enough has been said about email for other problems to be apparent. People sending personal messages can waste much time in an organisation. If this is done on a company heading or format there may be legal implications too; what happens if something is libellous? Thus organisations need firm policy and guidelines, and everyone needs to be disciplined in following the rules.

Some basic guidelines

As has been said, emails can be less formal than letters but still certain criteria as regards style and content are sensible (again an organisation may set out guidelines). Given the volume of emails people receive, you are competing for attention and must compose emails that are effective. An email should be:

- **Brief** - use plain words.
- **Direct** - clear presentation, no ambiguity.
- **Logical** - with a clear structure.

Whether emails are being sent internally or externally, as a substitute for a letter or not, it is important to ensure these rules are observed. A clear subject heading will make its purpose apparent and it may also be helpful to flag any (real!) urgency and say whether, and perhaps when, a reply is sought. Remember that email can, like any communication, have many intentions – to inform, persuade etc.

Before sending an email, considering the following will help ensure that it is presented effectively:

- What is the **objective** or purpose of email? Do you know what you are trying to achieve? Is the email a request for information? Are you circulating standard information? If the email is a quick response to a query, make sure that what you say is correct. If you are unsure, explain that this is an acknowledgement of receipt, and you will come back to them with more as soon as you can, preferably saying exactly when. If you do not know what the objective is, think carefully before sending your communication.

- What is the **background** to the issue? Is the reason for sending the email something that is to do with a problem in a project? Is there an explanation, excuse or apology required? Is it to elicit more information or to provide detailed answers to a query? For an email to be clearly understood, it must be apparent why you are sending it. If you don't know, check before writing it.

- Who is the intended **recipient?** Will it reach them direct, or be read by another person? Email inboxes are not necessarily only opened by the person named in the 'Send to' box. It is possible that colleagues have access to a person's mailbox, for example when someone is sick or on holiday. It is important to bear this in mind when writing a message, in case of issues.

- What **style** are you using? How is it being presented? Is the style really informal? Are you replying to a message which was replete with lots of missing capital letters, text message style shortened words, emoticons and the like? If so, that is fine. But think carefully what impression the style of the email gives to someone who is opening a communication from you for the first time or who thinks of you in a particular way.

- Choice of **content**. What is the email saying and is it being clearly communicated without any vagueness and ambiguity? Much has been said about this in earlier chapters. If the email covers complex matters, it may be better to explain that a document follows. It is usually intended for emails to be read quickly, and the content should reflect this.
- Is there a **conclusion** /recommendation /response required? If so, is this obvious? It may be clearest to place any request for action at the end of the email. Also by saying something like, *It would be helpful if you could bring this information with you when we meet at 4pm,* you give the recipient a clear message that they have until 4pm to complete the task. Finishing off an email with a direct instruction, or repeating the purpose of the message, will leave the reader in no doubt of your intention.
- What, if any, attachments are being sent? Specify any attachments clearly. If a device is used to 'squash' information together, such as zip files, it is always helpful to say it is attached as such. Some attachments can take ages to download and it is helpful to prewarn the recipient.

Putting yourself across appropriately in an email is important, especially because it is instant and non-retrievable. As with other written communication, there is no tone of voice, facial expression, posture, body language or gestures to augment your message. As email is a rapid and concise form of communication the detail matters. These are some of the most important points of detail to remember:

- *Format* – Use an appropriate format or house style. Make sure it matches the style used in the company's documents and check what other aspects of layout are standardised.

- *Typography / font* – Make sure you use a standard font, such as Times or Arial, and font size. You can also highlight key text using **bold**, <u>underline</u> and *italic*. Remember that reading on screen is not as easy as from paper – so make sure your chosen typeface is legible.

- *Subject* – Writer reference, case number or project name. This is just a polite way of ensuring that the recipient can save time by knowing what the email refers to. If you are sending an email to someone about a particular matter, it is helpful if they understand immediately what the message is about.

- *Salutation* – Are you on first name terms? Do you need to write in a more formal style because you have not exchanged correspondence before? Do you know the name of the person to whom you are writing or must you use an impersonal salutation?

- *Punctuation* – Beware ambiguity. A missing comma or no full stop can often cause confusion. If the reader is left puzzled by the meaning you are less likely to get a useful exchange of information.

- *Line length* – Short sentences and paragraphs, usually no more than 3-4 lines, make for easier reading on screen. Do not use complex sentences or syntax. Short and sweet is best.

- *Consistency* – If the email contains numbering take care. It is extremely irritating if the numbering changes in style or is inconsistent. If you are making a number of points, stick to a) b) c) or 1), 2) and 3).

- *Valediction* - Unlike a formal letter you don't have to sign off yours faithfully or yours sincerely. Many people use *kind regards, many thanks* and *best wishes* etc.

- *Details of the writer* such as title and company. Most email now have a 'default' signature, which ends the message. This includes your name and title as well as details of the organisation you represent (always include your phone number as well so the recipient can call you if preferred).

- *Attachments* – As mentioned before, these should be clearly described and mentioned in the text.

Note: While these points are especially important in context of the email, they overlap with the general principles of what makes any written message effective as dealt with earlier.

Digital Signatures and other security devices

Space prohibits going into detail about such things as encryption, but several other things should be noted with regard to security:

- *Encryption* is a special way to send sensitive information by email. It is a form of electronic code. One code is used to encrypt the message and another code is used to decrypt it. One key is private, and the other is public. The public key is passed to whoever needs to use it, whether they are sending the message (in which case they would use it for encryption) or if they are receiving the email (they would use it to decrypt the message). There is a wide range of information that you might consider disguising in this way. Such ranges from an account number to the fact that your company is launching a radical new product on a certain date.
- *Read Reports*: Some email systems allow a note to be shown when an email has been sent, received, opened and read by the recipient. This can be important in some time-critical instances. Alternatively, just ask for acknowledgement. This is obviously key when deadlines are involved; for example, I always ask for acknowledgement when submitting material for an article or book.

Losing any document can be a disaster. It is advisable, therefore, *to regularly back up* your files and data to safeguard against such risks. If passwords are used in your computer system, consider changing them on a regular basis to stop hackers and avoid misappropriation. There may be organisational guidelines about this, indeed about backing up your whole computer; but the responsibility for implementation is often likely to be personal.

Now to language (again with points that may be valid and useful beyond email).

Language and email

We have already touched on the lack of formality of many email messages. But clarity is essential and many messages must look and sound good – too much informality can dilute professionalism. So, remember: spell-check your emails when necessary and be aware of easily confused words. As an example of the dangers, consider a message saying:

After further consideration I have decided that your request for a salary increase of £10,000 per annum will now be agreed.

Try that sentence again inserting the word *not* instead of *now*...

There is a good deal elsewhere here about pure writing skills, so suffice it to say here that you should avoid:

- *Over complexity* (*From time to time* instead of *occasionally, it is necessary that* instead of *must*).
- *Unnecessarily long words* (*anticipate* instead of expect, *requirement* instead of *need*).
- *Overlong sentences*.

All such things make the essentially simple email unwieldy and less likely to do a good job.

Jargon and acronyms

Let's face it, everything seems to attract abbreviations; writers say that I am at the BOSHOK stage of writing this book – Bum on seat, hands on keyboard. Emails particularly seem to attract abbreviations. Those containing jargon, text language and acronyms (where initial letters are used to make up another word) are more likely to be confusing. However, because of email's overriding informality it is a good idea to be familiar with those that are universally used and note new ones are springing up daily, for instance FYI – for your information – is typical. Others may relate to your organisation, profession or industry sector. Beware using such in emails that are being sent externally where the recipient may not understand them; it is sometimes courteous to use full terminology in parenthesis afterwards.

Attachments

Email is made infinitely more useful because documents and files can be attached. Attachments can include word documents, images, sound or video files. It is even possible to email computer programs.

Sometimes it may help to compress files that are being sent as email attachments. This will reduce the upload time while transmitting the information. It also speeds up the download time for you if someone sends you a large file that has already been zipped.

The advantage of sending documents and files as attachments is the speed and efficiency of communications. The recipient of the documents will be able to keep these on file and can move, edit, return or forward them on as necessary. If security is an issue, an attachment should be sent in PDF format, preventing the document being edited by the recipient (though they can be printed). This is usually safe and secure for sensitive material.

Hyperlinks

Inserting hyperlinks into email messages is particularly useful when sending information to people. If something that is available on a webpage needs to be communicated to your recipient (of which you do not have a copy), simply insert the *hyperlink* into the email message. The recipient simply clicks on the link to open the web page. Remember doing this takes time, some people may not bother; so, for instance, information sent this way to a customer as a part of a total message might thus never be seen and dilute the intended effect. It is, however, a good way to attract further engagement.

Potential problems

Email, and the Internet on which it is dependent, can pose some serious problems: spam, viruses and the time-wasting inherent in managing email files inefficiently are widely known and this is not the place to list details and remedies (though it is worth saying that care is necessary and guidelines within an organisation about security etc. should be strictly followed). To start to summarise, here are a few do's and don'ts and points going a little beyond the writing of these electronic messages.

Don't
- Send emails just because they are easy.
- Enter text IN CAPITAL LETTERS. It is taken as shouting.
- Use them as a substitute for properly delegating a task to another.
- Send them to discharge yourself of responsibility.
- Put something in an email that is confidential, it can be abused.
- Forward someone's email if they asked you not to.
- Assume your recipient wanted it and is desperate to receive it.

Do

- Think and use the "send later" or "draft" button to inject some thinking time.
- Be precise, to reduce clarification emails and phone calls.
- Reply promptly. Because email is quick, a rapid reply is generally expected.
- Be polite and friendly but never assume familiarity with jargon.
- Keep attachments to a minimum.
- Avoid gobbledygook.

That said, here are some final tips to end this chapter.

Ten basic tips for better email technique

1. **Use email as one channel of communication, but not the only one.** This is important; do not be lazy just because it is fast and easy. Emails can document discussions and send high impact messages around the world at the click of a mouse. But they can also mislead managers into thinking they can communicate with large groups of people solely through regular group emails. Use email widely but only as one of a range of management tools. It's not possible to reach everyone, and the 'impersonal' non-direct contact means that people can feel slighted by the loss of the personal touch.
2. **It pays to keep it short and sweet.** Emails that are longer than a full screen tend not to be read straight away. They get left till later and often not until the end of the day or beyond. It is important to judge when it is right to put down the mouse and seek the person out face-to-face, or just phone them. Certainly, never let brevity and clarity compete and brevity win.
3. **Communicate clearly – cut out the codes.** Email requires clarity of purpose. Be sure your message comes

across without any doubt or misunderstanding. Also it is important to be sure to whom your message needs to be addressed, and who really needs a copy for information. In terms of actions and priorities, use lists or bullet points for clarity. Response buttons (or similar) should be used if you need to see who has received and read your message.

4. **Encourage open communication** when using email, request people to respond with questions or queries if they wish. It shows that you are concerned and available to help.

5. **Do not use emails to get mad with people.** Far better to save anger for face-to-face encounters (where facial expression and body language can be used to great effect) or over the phone where tone of voice can speak volumes. Sarcasm, irony, criticism or venom are not appropriate when sending emails. Certainly it is difficult to project such feelings clearly, and messages can come over as far more harsh than you intended.

6. **Humour should be used with caution.** By all means use wit and humour to lighten a heavy atmosphere but emoticons, smiley faces and joke emails are not usually appropriate in the work environment. Some companies ban joke emails; they are too risky and may erode your attempts to send serious ones.

7. **Suspend reaction – use the 5-minute rule.** It is often wise to delay sending a hastily written email for five minutes (or more!) before pressing the 'send' button. If you are angry or upset when you write something, it is a good idea to take a break or do something else before writing. If you do write the message, once you have cooled off take a moment to review it before sending it out.

8. **Set aside time to deal with emails.** Because of the growing importance of emails as a percentage of the total number of messages you receive, you need to make time to deal with them; if this demands reconfiguring your working day – so be it.

9. **Take advantage of language.** To avoid errors and complicated sentences, use words carefully to ensure clarity of communication accompanies the brevity so beloved of email writers.

CHAPTER 6

ON YOUR FEET

The golden rule for presenters
is to imagine that you are in the audience.

David Martin

PRESENTING SUCCESSFULLY: THE BUSINESS EQUIVALENT OF AN OPEN GOAL

Next the essentials of the skills of presenting are reviewed. Most of what makes for a good presentation is common sense, though there is a degree of organisation – perhaps orchestration is a better word – involved. Always remember that presenting puts you in a powerful position. If you can calm any nerves that threaten to interfere, then you can think positively about it and that will help you achieve what you want.

A SIGNIFICANT OPPORTUNITY

It is precisely because of this that presentations present a real opportunity. If you can do them well (and you can) then you will positively differentiate yourself from others, who from ignorance or lack of care, do an undistinguished or poor job.

It is worth quoting here a phrase used in a training film about making presentations, where a character describes presentations as being the *business equivalent of an open goal*. Well put; this is not overstating the point and puts it in a memorable way (I quote from the excellent film *I wasn't prepared for that*, produced by Video Arts Limited).

So, motivation should not be in doubt here. There are few business skills more worth mastering than that of presentation; without them you not only feel exposed, you *are* exposed. The trouble is the ground does not mercifully open up and allow you to disappear along with your embarrassment, it is more likely that the result is much more real – no agreement, no commitment or the boss saying ominously: *See me afterwards*.

There are good reasons for having fears, but all can either be overcome or reduced to stop them overpowering your ability to work successfully. It may help to think of things as a balance. On one side there are things that can, unless dealt with, reduce your ability to make a good presentation. On the other there are techniques that positively assist the process. The right attention to both sides improves your capability.

Much here is about the positive techniques. But let us start with a little more about possible difficulties, some of which are inherent to the process, and how to overcome them – if only to get the negative side out of the way first.

THE AUDIENCE'S NIGHTMARE

Before anything else let's consider what modern technology has done to the preparation and delivery of presentations. You may well attend more presentations than you give, so imagine for a moment that you are in the audience:

The presenter stands at the front of the room, surrounded

by equipment and with the screen glowing behind them. The audience is spellbound. The little company logo at the corner of the screen fascinates them. Every time the presenter clicks the computer mouse, and sends another yellow bullet point shuttling onto the screen from stage left, their attention veritably soars. One slide replaces another, then another replaces that and then another in a bonanza of bullet points... but you get the idea. Enough. Too often all are bland, all lengthy sentences, yet the presenter who must be listened to finds them riveting; certainly they spend most of their time looking over their shoulder at the screen rather than at the audience.

There is so much text on some slides that they are like pages out of a book. And an unsuitably small typeface compounds the effect and overburdens the minds of the audience. So the presenter aims to improve this by reading from them, verbatim, more slowly than the audience does and with a tone that leads one to suspect that they are seeing them for the first time. It becomes akin to a bureaucratic rain dance: a mantra and format is slavishly, indeed unthinkingly, followed - yet at the end no one is truly satisfied. Any opportunity that might have existed is at best diluted, at worst missed.

Both presenter and audience have suffered the now ubiquitous "death by PowerPoint".

It gets relentless, more so when they contain lengthy sentences:

Look at this interesting bullet point just going up on the screen now to illustrate what I'm saying, or rather to duplicate what I say because what I am actually doing is reading it to you as I...

Sometimes such sentences fill the entire screen. Enough – if only good business presentations were that easy, so mechanistic. Put up one slide, read its text out loud – repeat, and success follows automatically.

But they are not.

Large numbers of lacklustre, wordy slides do not a good presentation make. Certainly they do not make it distinctive or memorable. But then perhaps, honestly assessed, the kind of presenter caricatured above does not really believe they do. The slides are there – be honest – because *that is how presentations are prepared and delivered*. A ubiquitous norm is followed largely unthinkingly, and the results fail to sparkle (at worst the "death by PowerPoint"). Indeed they may fail to explain, inform and certainly to persuade.

There has to be a better way.

Indeed, there is. Much can be done to avoid a presentation becoming bland and lacklustre. The approaches and ideas that follow can be used or adapted to enliven what you do and maximise its effectiveness. But PowerPoint, for all its many strengths, is not the only hazard, so we will get some negatives out of the way first and suggest how they can be overcome.

THE HAZARDS OF BEING "ON YOUR FEET"

Presenting can be daunting and people sometimes say of a presentation that they know they could fluently go through the content if they were instead sat comfortably opposite just one other person.

The first rule here is easy. Ease of communication should never be taken for granted. As has already been said, it needs thought, care, and precision and this is doubly so when you present formally. With most presentations you only get one crack at it, and often there is not the to and fro nature of conversation that is sometimes necessary to establishes understanding.

This means every tiny detail matters. Presentations are inherently fragile. Small differences – an ill-chosen word or phrase, a hesitation, a misplaced emphasis – can all too easily act to dilute the impact sought.

At least communication problems constitute a tangible factor. If you resolve to take care your presentations will work and understanding (and acceptance) will be more certain. You can work at getting this right. Many of the elements reviewed as this section continues assist this process, but what about less tangible fears?

Presenters' nightmares

Whatever you fear will make making a presentation more difficult, it is probable that others think the same. Asking groups on workshops I conduct on the subject about their worries usually produces a very similar list of factors.

The top ten, in no particular order, are as follows.

1. **Butterflies in the stomach:** if you are nervous, then you are likely to look nervous. Without *some* apprehension, which can act to focus you on the job in hand, you would probably not do so well. Much of this feeling will fade as you get underway (and, with experience, knowing this will help too), but you can help the process in a number of ways, for instance:

2.

    • Taking some deep breaths before you start (nerves tend to make you breathe more shallowly and starve you of oxygen), and remember to breathe as you go along (running out of breath to the point of gasping is a surprisingly common fault).
    • Taking a sip of water just before you start.
    • Not eating a heavy meal before a presentation.
    • Nor eating nothing (or rumbles may join the butterflies).
    • Alcohol really does not help; at worst it may persuade you that you can do something you cannot and make matters worse as the truth dawns.

3. **A dry mouth:** is easily cured. Take a sip of water. Never attempt to speak without a glass of water in front of you. Even if you do not touch it, knowing it is there is a comfort.

4. **Not knowing what to do with your hands:** The best solution is to give them something to do – hold the lectern, a pencil or the remote control for your slides, make the occasional gesture – but then forget about them. *Thinking* about them as you proceed will make matters worse.

5. **Not knowing how loud to speak:** Just imagine you are speaking to the furthest person in the room (if they were the only one there you would have little problem judging volume); better still test it beforehand whenever this is possible.

6. **A hostile reaction:** The vast majority of groups want it to go well. They are disposed to be on your side. The only thing worse than knowing that you are not presenting well is being in the audience; think about it.

7. **Not having sufficient material:** This can be removed completely as a fear; if your presentation is well prepared you will *know* there is the right amount.

8. **Having too much material:** As point 6; enough said for the moment.

9. **Losing your place:** Also tied in with preparation (and something else reviewed in detail elsewhere). Your notes should be organised specifically so that it is unlikely that you will lose your place (and so that you can find it easily should you do so).

10. **Drying up:** Why should this happen? Dry mouth? Take a sip of water. Lose your place? Organise it so that this does not happen. Or is it just nerves? Well some of the factors already mentioned will help – so too will preparation. And if it does happen, often it takes only a second to resume: *There was another point here, ah yes, the questions of ...* The problem here can be psychological; it just *feels* as if you paused forever.

11. **Misjudging the timing:** This is something else speakers' notes can help with specifically.

All that is necessary for so many such problems or thoughts is a practical response, something that acts certainly to remove or reduce the adverse effect. Thinking of it this way helps too. Try not to worry. No doom and gloom. It will be more likely to go well if you are sure it will – more so if you work at organising so that every factor helps.

However, few people can speak without thought. It was the author Mark Twain who said:

It usually takes me three weeks to prepare a good impromptu speech.

Preparation is key to success and it's to that which we turn to next.

PREPARING TO PRESENT

This topic is also dealt with in Chapter 2. Imagine that you have a presentation to make. Maybe you have one to be done soon (if not, bear in mind that this is a task that so many jobs do not allow you to avoid). Few people will simply do nothing about it until the day and then get up and speak. So what do you do? Let us address some dangers first to lead into what is best practice here. What you might do is think of what you want to say first, then think of what follows – what you will say second, third and so on – and then write it down verbatim. Or, more commonly, write it down in chunks that just fit PowerPoint slides; the first act of preparation is most often to sit at the computer and open PowerPoint. Then, perhaps after some judicious amendment, you read it to the group you must address.

Wrong, wrong and wrong again.

This might sound logical, but contains the seeds of disaster.

Do not try to read verbatim

Why should you not? Well, first you will find it is really very difficult to read anything smoothly, get all the emphasis exactly where it needs to be, and do so fluently and without stumbling. The actors that record audio novels deserve their money: real skill is involved.

Most people speak very much better from notes that are an abbreviation of what they intend to say. If you doubt this, just try it – read something out loud and see how it sounds; better still record it and *hear* how it sounds. In addition, certainly in a business context, you rarely need to be able to guarantee so exact a form of wording (there are exceptions, of course, a key definition or description may need to be word perfect). It is usually more important to ensure the emphasis, variety and pace is right and that is what is so difficult to achieve when reading.

Having established that, preparation needs to facilitate being able to present in a more fluid and fluent manner; that starts with objectives.

Clear purpose

Rarely, if ever, will you be asked just to "talk about" something. The most crucial question any intending presenter can ask themselves is simply:

Why is this presentation to be made?

If you can answer that clearly, it will be easier both to prepare and present. Let us be clear here:

Objectives are not what you intend to say, rather they should describe what you intend to achieve.

Apologies if this seems obvious, but I have regularly observed presentations (often carefully prepared and brought to training workshops in the knowledge that they will be subject to critique), which are poor almost solely because they have no clear objectives. They rattle along reasonably well; but they do not actually *go* anywhere. Objectives are therefore fundamental – and details about setting them were reviewed elsewhere.

At this point we might logically focus for a while on the audience; after all, no audience, no presentation.

Your audience

Everything is easier with a clear view of your audience. First, who are they? They may be people you know, men/women, expert or inexperienced about whatever topic you must address; there are many permutations here. Most important, however, are the *audience's expectations* – what do they want?

Put yourself in their place. Facing a presentation, what do you say to yourself? Most people anticipate its impact on them – *Will this be interesting, useful, long or short; what will this person be like, will I want to listen to them, how will what they have to say help me?* Again the permutations are many (though usually not too complicated to think through), but bearing audience viewpoint in mind is a major factor in ensuring a successful outcome.

Specifically, any audience *wants* you to:

- "Know your stuff."
- Look the part.
- Respect them, acknowledging their situation and their views.
- Flag links between what you say and what they want from the talk.
- Give an adequate message: so that they understand and can weigh up whether they agree with what is said or not (this is especially important if you are going to suggest or demand action of them).
- Make it "right for them" (for example, in terms of level of technicality).
- Hold their attention and interest throughout.

It is equally important to consider what audiences *do not want,* which includes their *not* being:

- Confused.
- Blinded with science, technicalities or jargon.

- Lost in a convoluted structure (or because there is none).
- Made to struggle to understand inappropriate language.
- Made to stretch to relate what is said to their own circumstances.
- Made to listen to someone who, by being ill prepared, shows no respect for the group.

A good presenter will always have empathy for the group they address; and that must be evident to them. Often this is something guided by prior knowledge. But it can, of course, vary; you may well need to speak to groups you do not know well. Always find out what you can about them and make use of everything you discover.

How the group sees a presenter

Clearly how you start matters – first impressions last as they say – and we come to this later. Also you must not just be well-organised, you must *look* well-organised. Walking to the front, however confidently, is likely to be spoiled if you are clutching a bulging folder spilling papers in all directions, and start by saying, *I am sure I have the first slide here somewhere* accompanied by fevered mouse clicks and a kaleidoscope of images as you attempt to find it.

Any business presenter must direct the group, must be in charge, and must therefore look the part. Certainly appearance in this sense is important, though it should link to the culture and circumstances in which the presentation takes place. Similarly, you should normally stand up (there may be some sessions that can be presented while sitting, but these are less common). Most people will actually perform in a different and more stimulating manner when standing – it somehow gets the adrenaline flowing. If standing is the chosen option, stand up straight, neither stand stock still or move about too much, and aim to present an appearance of purposefulness.

The speaker is the expert, and is, or should be, in charge,

and so appearance is a relevant factor. Audiences tend to make positive assumptions based on first impressions *provided these are good*.

How you see the audience

How you view the group is not, of course, simply a visual point; what is necessary is an understanding of the group, and the individuals in it, and an appreciation of their point of view and their way of seeing things. Presentations may well demand decisions of people: *Do I agree? Can I see the relevance of this? Shall I agree with this point?* So it is necessary to understand – be empathetic – and anyone making a presentation must not simply talk *at* their audience, but rather tailor their approach based on an understanding of the audience's point of view.

Now remembering all this, one of the dangers is at once apparent. This is that the other person's point of view can be neglected, or ignored, with the presenter focusing primarily, or only, on their own point of view. You should ensure that you do not become introspective, concerned with your own views or situation; but instead use and display enough empathy to come over as being constantly concerned about others' views. This sounds obvious, but it is all too easy to find your own perspective predominating, thus creating a dilution of effectiveness. Even the most important message has to earn a hearing, and this is achieved primarily through concentrating on what is important to the group. Nervousness of the actual process of presenting may compound this potential danger.

Next, before we turn to the structure of the presentation itself and review how one goes through it, let's focus specifically on preparation again.

Preparation: the key tasks

A much-quoted maxim about any kind of communication is the saying *"Tell'em, tell'em and tell'em"*. This can be stated more clearly as meaning that you should tell people what you are going to tell them, tell them and then tell them what it was you told them. This may sound silly, but compare it with something a little different, the way a good report is set out, for instance. There is an introduction, which says what follows; there is the main body of the document, which goes progressively through the message; and the summary which, well, summarises or says what has been covered. The idea is straightforward, but if it is ignored, messages may then go largely to waste.

Having mentioned structure, let's acknowledge that it's preparation that creates your beginning, middle and end and everything else along the way.

The key issues are to:

- Be able to answer the question: Why must this presentation be made? And have a clear purpose in mind, one that reflects the audience and the effect you want to have on them.
- Decide *what* to say (and what not to say).
- Arrange things in a logical order
- Think about *how* it will be put over (not just the pure content, but examples, anecdotes and any element of humour).
- Prepare suitable notes as an aide memoir to have in front of you as you speak (but not, as has been said, to read verbatim); slides alone may not be enough – if you rely on these as *your reference* they will likely be too full of text. However, a paper copy of slides, with added notes and emphasis works well.
- Anticipate reactions and questions and how you will deal with these.

All this must be done with a keen eye on the planned duration of the presentation so that what you prepare fits (you may need to decide the time length, you may be told the duration or have to ask what is suitable). Finishing on time always impresses (and running over may get you cut off or put someone acting as Chair into a very bad mood).

What you should prepare is speaker's notes. Do *not*, as I have said, start with slides – slides *support what you say,* they should not lead. Now clearly your guiding notes should follow a clear structure, but if you have some sensible thoughts about notes then you can more easily imagine the structure fitting onto that format.

YOUR SPEAKER'S NOTES

For most people having *something* in front of them as they speak is essential. The question is what form exactly should it take? Speaker's notes have several roles, to:

- Boost confidence: in the event you may not need everything that is in front of you, but knowing it's there is, in itself, useful.
- Act as a guide to what you will say, in what order and duration.
- Assist you say it in the best possible way: producing the right variety, pace, emphasis etc. as you go along.

Conversely notes must not act as a straitjacket and stifle all possibility of flexibility. After all, what happens if your audience's interest suggests a digression or more detail before proceeding? Or the reverse, if a greater level of prior information or experience becomes apparent meaning that you want to recast or abbreviate something you plan to say? Or if, as you get up to speak for half an hour, the person in the Chair whispers: *Can you keep it to twenty minutes? We are running a bit behind.* Good notes should assist with these and other scenarios as well.

Again there is no intention here to be comprehensive, rather I set out some tried and tested approaches, not for you to follow slavishly but as a prompt to evolving a way that suits you. Do note, however, that there is advantage in adopting (if not immediately) a consistent approach to how you work here. This can act to make preparation more certain and you are more likely also to become quicker and quicker at getting your preparation done if you do so.

The format of notes

The following might be adopted as **rules**:

- Legibility is essential (you must use a sufficiently large typeface, or writing, avoid adding tiny, untidy embellishments and remember that notes must be suitable to be used standing up and therefore at a greater distance from your eyes than if you sat to read them).
- The materials must be well chosen – for you. Some people favour small cards, others larger sheets. A standard A4 ring binder works well (one with a pocket at the front may be useful for ancillary items you may want with you). Whatever you choose make sure it *lies flat*. It is certain to be disconcerting if a folded page turns back on itself – especially if you repeat a whole section. It can happen!
- Using only one side of the paper allows space for amendment and addition if necessary and/or makes the total package easier to follow (some people like notes arranged with slides reproduced alongside to produce a comprehensive double-page spread).
- Always page number your material (yes, one day, as sure as eggs are eggs, you will drop it). Some people like to number the pages in reverse order – 10, 9, 8 etc. – which gives some guidance regarding time remaining until the end. Decide which – and stick with one way to avoid confusion.
- Separate different types of note: for example *what you intend to say* and *how* (emphasis etc.).

- Use colour and symbols to help you find your way, yet minimise what must be noted.

The detail on the speaker's notes needs to be just sufficient for a well-prepared speaker to be able to work from it and do so comfortably. Consider the devices mentioned here, and try to imagine the effect that the use of a second (or third?) colour would have on its ease of use – some highlighting is clearly more dramatic in fluorescent yellow, for example.

Consider the following ideas: there should be things here you can copy or adapt, or which prompt additional ideas that suit you:

- **Main divisions:** The pages – imagine they are A4 – are divided (a coloured line is best) into smaller segments, each creating a manageable area on which the eye can focus with ease; this helps ensure that you don't lose your place (effectively it produces something of the effect of using cards rather than sheets).
- **Symbols** which save space and visually jump off the page making sure you do not miss them. It is best to avoid possible confusion by always using the same symbol to represent the same thing and maybe also to restrict the overall number used; a plethora of them might become difficult to follow. Use bold exclamation marks etc. and **S1** (Slide 1) etc. to show which slide is shown where there are examples.
- **Columns:** These separate different elements of the notes. Clearly there are various options here in terms of number of columns and what goes where.
- **Space:** Turning over only takes a second (often you can end a page where a slight pause is necessary anyway). It's always best to give yourself plenty of space, not least to facilitate amendments and, of course, to allow individual elements to stand out.

- **Emphasis:** This must be as clear as content; again a second colour helps.
- **Timing:** An indication of time elapsed (or still to go) can be included little or often as you find useful; remember the audience love to have time commitments kept.
- **Options:** This term is used to describe points included as a separate element and as such can be particularly useful. Options can be added or omitted depending on such factors as time and feedback. They help fine-tune the final delivery and are good for confidence. They might go in a third righthand column.

Note that points in the "Options" column are designed to be included or not, depending on the situation. A plan might thus include ten points under options with half of them (regardless of which) making your total presentation up to the planned duration. Thus you can extend or decrease to order and fluently work in additional material where more detail (or an aside for example) seems appropriate on the day.

Note: The pages of your notes may be printed versions of your slides with notations added. That works well and many people operate that way. Some detailed notes about slides form the last section of this chapter.

Good preparation and good notes go together. If you are well prepared, confident of your material and confident also that you have a really clear guide in front of you, then you are well on the way to making a good presentation.

PREPARATION CONCLUDED

A final look (perhaps after a break following preparation) is always valuable. This is also the time to consider rehearsal, either talking it through to yourself, to a tape recorder or colleague, or having a full scale "dress rehearsal".

If you are speaking as part of a team, *always* make sure that speakers get together ahead of the event to rehearse, or at least discuss, both any possible overlaps and any necessary handover between speakers. You are seeking to create what appears to the audience to be a seamless transition between separate contributors. Any rehearsal you decide is necessary should be done: thoroughly, sufficiently far ahead and given sufficient time.

Thereafter, depending on the nature of the presentation, it may be useful – or necessary – to spend more time, either in revision or just reading over what you plan to do. You should not overdo revision at this stage; however, there comes a time to simply be content you have it right and stick with it.

This whole preparation process is important and not to be skimped. Preparation does get easier however. You will find that, with practice, you begin to produce material that needs less amendment and that both getting it down and any subsequent revision begin to take less time.

At the end of the day, as has been said, you need to find your own version of the procedures set out here. A systematic approach helps, but the intention is not to over-engineer the process. What matters is that you are comfortable with your chosen approach, and that it works for you. If this is the case then, provided it remains consciously designed to achieve what is necessary, it will become a habit. It will need less thinking about, yet still act to guarantee that you turn out something that you are content meets your needs - whatever they may be.

Now (at last) we consider the presentation stage by stage and start, with appropriate logic, at the beginning, and see how you can get to grips with that.

THE STRUCTURE OF A PRESENTATION

The beginning

The beginning is clearly an important stage. Remember people are uncertain; they are saying to themselves: *What will this be like? Will I find it interesting/helpful*? They may also have their minds on other matters: what is going on back at the office, with the job they left half finished, and more. This is particularly true when the people in the group do not know you, or know you well. They then have little or no previous experience of what to expect, and this will condition their thinking (and maybe some previous experience will make them wary!). With people you know well there is less of a problem, but the first moments of any speech are nevertheless always important.

The beginning is not only important to the participants, it is also important to the presenter; nothing settles the nerves – and even the most experienced speakers usually have a few qualms before they start – better than making a good start. Remember, the beginning is, necessarily, the introduction; the main objective is therefore to set the scene, state the topic (and rationale for it) clearly, and begin to discuss the 'meat' of the content. In addition, you have to obtain the group's attention – they will never take the message onboard if they are not concentrating and taking in what goes on – and create some sort of rapport between you and the group, and secondly around the group itself.

Let us take these aspects in turn:

1. Gaining attention

This is primarily achieved by your manner and by the start you make. You have to look the part; your manner has to say: *This will be interesting, this person knows what they are talking about*. A little has been said about such factors as appearance, standing up, and so on. Suffice to say here that if your start appears hesitant, the wrong impression will be given and everything thereafter will be more difficult. Most important is what you say first and how it is said.

There are a number of types of opening, each presenting a range of opportunities for differing lead-ins. For example:

- *A question*: rhetorical or otherwise, preferably something that people are likely to respond to positively: *Would you welcome a better way to…?*
- *A quotation*: which might be humorous or make a point, which might be a classic or novel phrase; or it might be something internal: *At the last company meeting, the M.D. said…*
- *A story*: again, something that makes a point, relates to the situation or people, or draws on a common memory: *We all remember the situation at the end of the last financial year when…*
- *A factual statement*: perhaps striking, thought-provoking, challenging or surprising: *Do you realise that this company receives 120 complaints every working day? (*The fact that this is also a question indicates that all these methods and more can be linked).
- *A dramatic statement*: a story with a startling end, perhaps. Or a statement that surprises in some way. For instance, once, talking about direct mail advertising, I started by asking the group to count, out loud and in unison from 1-10. Between two and three I banged my fist down on the table saying *Stop!* loudly. *And that*, I continued, *is how long your direct mail has to catch people's attention – 2½ seconds!*
- *A historical fact*: a reference back to an event that is a common experience of the group: '*Last year, when company sales for what was then a new product were just…*'
- *A curious opening*: simply a statement sufficiently odd for people to wait to find what on earth it is all about: *Consider the aardvark, and how it shares a characteristic of some of our managers…* (In case you want the link, it is thick skinned).
- *A checklist*: perhaps a good start when placing the

'shopping list' in mind early on is important: *There are 10 key stages to the process we want to discuss, first…*

There must be more methods and combinations of methods that you can think of.

Whatever way you pick, this element of the session needs careful, and perhaps very precise, preparation.

2.   Creating rapport

At the same time, you need to ensure that an appropriate group feeling is started. In terms of what you say (participation also has a role here), you may want to set a patterns of 'we' rather than 'them and us'; in other words, say, '*We need to consider…*' and not '*You must…*' If this approach is followed then a more comfortable atmosphere is created: you may add – discreetly – a compliment or two: '*As experienced people, you will…*', though without over boasting; above all, *be enthusiastic*. It is said that the one good aspect of life that is infectious is enthusiasm. Use it.

At the same time, the opening stages need to make it absolutely clear what the objectives are, what will be dealt with, and how it will benefit those present. It must also move us into the topic in a constructive way.

This opening stage is the first "Tell'em" from "Tell'em, tell'em and tell'em".

The middle

The middle is the core of the session. The objectives are clear:

*   To put over the detail of the message.
*   Ensure acceptance of the message.
*   Maintain attention throughout the process.

You also need to anticipate, prevent and, if necessary, handle any possible objections.

One of the principles here is to take one point at a time; we shall do just that here, under four headings:

1.   Putting over the content

The main trick here is to adopt a structured approach. Make sure you are dealing with points in a logical sequence; for instance, working through a process in a chronological order. And use 'signposting', that goes straight back to the three 'tell'ems'; you cannot say things like *'There are three key points here; performance, method and cost; let's deal with them in turn. First, performance ....'* too much. Give advance warning of what is coming (this applies to both content and the nature of what is being said. Saying *'For example ...'* is a simple form of signposting. It makes it clear what you are doing and makes it clear also that you are not moving onto the next content point just yet.) Putting everything in context, and relating it to a planned sequence of delivery, keeps the message organised and improves understanding.

This technique, and the clarity it helps produce give you the overall effect you want. People must obviously understand what you are talking about. There is no room for verbosity, for too much jargon, or for anything that clouds understanding. One pretty good measure of the presenter is when people afterwards feel that, perhaps for the first time, they really have come to clearly understand something that has just been explained.

In presenting, a spade has to be called a spade. What is more, it has, as it were, to be an interesting spade if it is to be referred to at all and if attention is to be maintained.

2.   Maintaining attention

Here again the principles are straightforward.

Keep stressing the relevance of what is being discussed

to the audience. For instance, do not just say that some matter will be a cost saving to the organisation, stress personal benefits – will it make something easier, quicker or more satisfying to do, perhaps?

Make sure that the presentation remains visually interesting by using visual aids and demonstrations wherever possible.

Use descriptions that incorporate stories, or anecdotes to make the message live. You cannot make a presentation live by formal content alone; you need an occasional anecdote, or something less formal. It is nice if you are able to both proceed through the content you must present and seemingly remain flexible, apparently digressing and adding in something interesting, a point that exemplifies or makes something more interesting as you go. How do you do this? It is back to preparation.

Finally, continue to generate attention through your own interest and enthusiasm.

3. Obtaining acceptance

People will only implement what they have come to believe is good sense. It is not enough to have put the message over and for it to be understood – it has to be *believed*.

Here we must start by going back to understanding; nothing will be truly accepted unless this is achieved. Note that to some extent better understanding is helped by:

- Using clear, precise language – language which is familiar to those present, and which does not over-use jargon.
- Making explanation clear, making no assumptions, using plenty of similes (you can hardly say '*this is like…*' too often), and with sufficient detail to get the point across. One danger here is that in explaining points that *you* know well, you start to abbreviate,

allowing your understanding to blind you as to how far back it is necessary to go with people for whom the message is new.

- Demonstration adds considerably to the chances of understanding. These can be specific: talk about products, for instance, and it may be worth showing one. In this case, the golden rule is (surprise, surprise) preparation. Credibility is immediately at risk if something is mentioned and needs visualising, yet cannot be. Help your audience's imagination and your message will go over better.

Visual aids are of course also a powerful aid to understanding.

Effectiveness is not, however, just a question of understanding. As has been said, acceptance is also vital. Acceptance is helped by factors already mentioned (telling people how something will benefit them – or others they are concerned about, such as their staff), and the more specific this link can be made the better the effect will be on the view formed.

Finally, it is worth making the point that you will not always know whether acceptance of a point has been achieved, unless you check. People cannot be expected to nod or speak out at every point, yet knowing that you have achieved acceptance may be important as you proceed. Questions to establish appropriate feedback are therefore necessary, and in some presentations this must be done as you progress. It is also advisable to keep an eye on the visible signs; watching, for instance, for puzzled looks.

4. Handling objections

The first aspect here is the anticipation, indeed the pre-emption, of objections. Sometimes it is clear that some subject to be dealt with is likely, even guaranteed, to produce a negative reaction. If there is a clear answer then it can be built into what you say, avoiding any waste of time. It may be as simple as a comment such as: '*Of course, this needs time, always a scarce resource, but once set up is done time will be saved regularly*', which then goes on to explain how this will happen.

Very importantly, never, ever bluff. If you do not know the answer you must say so (no group expects you to be infallible), and you may well have to find out the answer later and report back. Alternatively, *does anyone else know?* Similarly, even when you can answer, there is no harm in delaying a reply:

That's a good point, perhaps I can pick it up, in context, when we deal with…

A final word here: beware of digression. It is good to answer any ancillary points that come up, but you can stray too far. Part of the presenter's job is that of chairperson; everything planned for the session has to be covered, and before the scheduled finishing time. If therefore, you sometimes have to draw a close to a line of enquiry, make it clear that time is pressing. Do not ever let anyone feel it was a silly point to raise.

After all this, when we have been through the session, the time comes to wind up.

The end

Always end on a high note (something that may mean the last slide you show needs careful selection). The group expect it, if only subconsciously. It is an opportunity to build on past success during the session or, occasionally, to make amends for anything that has been less successful.

That apart, the end acts as a pulling together of the overall message that has been given. However you finally end, there is often a need to summarise in an orderly fashion. This may well be linked to an action plan for the future, so that in wrapping up what has been said is reviewed – completing the

"Tell'ems" – and a commitment is sought as to what should happen next. This is important. Most people are under pressure for time. They will be busier afterwards even having taken half an hour taken to sit through your presentation, so there is a real temptation to put everything on one side and get back to work – get back to normal. Yet this may be just where a little time needs to be put in to start to make some changes. Their having a real intention in mind as they leave the session is not a guarantee that action will flow, but it is a start. It makes it that much more likely that something will happen, especially if follow up action is taken to remind and see the matter through.

Like the beginning, there is then a need to find a way of handling the final signing off. You can, for instance, finish with:

- *A question*: that leaves the final message hanging in the air, or makes it more likely that people will go on thinking about the issues a little longer: *I asked a question at the start of the session, now let us finish with another...*

- *A quotation:* that encapsulates an important, or the last, point: '*Good communication is as stimulating as black coffee, and just as hard to sleep after* (Anne Morrow Lindberg),

- Alternatively, choose something that, while not linked inextricably to the topic, just makes a good closing line, for example: *The more I practice, the more good luck I seem to have (*which is attributed to many a famous golfer), is one that might suit something with training or instructional content.

- *A story*: longer than the quotation, but with the same sort of intention. If it is meant to amuse, be sure it does; you have no further chance at the end to retrieve the situation.

- *An alternative*: This may be as simple as: *Will you do this or not?* Or the more complicated option of a spelt-out plan, A, B, or C?

- *Immediate gain:*This is an injunction to act linked to an advantage of doing so now. *Put this new system in place and you will be saving time and money tomorrow'* – more fiercely phrased, it is called a fear-based end: *Unless you ensure this system is running you will not...* Although there is sometimes a place for the latter, the positive route is usually better.

However you decide to wrap things up, the end should be a logical conclusion, rather than something separate added to the end.

VISUAL AIDS

Perhaps the most important visual aid is unexpected: it is you. A number of factors, such as simple gestures (for example, a hand pointing), and more dramatic ones like banging a fist on the table, which may be described as flourishes, are part of this as is your general manner and appearance.

More tangible forms of visual aid are also important. Such things as slides serve several roles; these include:

- Focusing attention within the group.
- Helping chance pace, add variety etc.
- Giving a literally visual aspect to something.
- Acting as signposts to where within the structure the presentation has reached.

They also help the presenter, providing reminders over and above speaker's notes on what comes next. Be careful. Visual aids should *support* the message, not lead or take it over. Just because slides exist or are easy to originate (especially with PowerPoint) does not mean they will be right. You need to start by looking at the message, at what you are trying to do, and see what will help put it over and have an additive effect. They may make a point that is difficult or impossible to describe, in the way a graph might make an instant point which would be lost in a mass of figures. Or you may have a particular reason to use them; to help get a large amount of information over more quickly, perhaps.

The checklist that follows deals, briefly, with the various options, offers general guidance on visual aids, and some tips on using the ubiquitous PowerPoint:

General principles of using visual aids

- Keep the content simple.
- Restrict the amount of information and the number of words: use single words to give structure, headings, or short statements – avoid it looking cluttered or complicated – use a running logo (e.g. the main heading/ topic on each slide).
- Use diagrams, graphs etc. where possible rather than too many figures and never read figures aloud without visual support.
- Build in variety within the overall theme: e.g. with colour or variations of the form of aid used.
- Emphasise the theme and structure: e.g. regularly using a single aid to recap the agenda or objectives.
- Ensure the content of the visual matches the words spoken.
- Make sure content is necessary and relevant.
- Ensure everything is visible: asking yourself, Is it clear? Will it work in the room? Does it suit the equipment? Colours, and the right sized typeface (often too small) help here.
- Ensure the layout emphasises the meaning you want (and not some minor detail).
- Pick the right aid for the right purpose.

The ubiquitous Microsoft PowerPoint system (and other systems) allows you to prepare slides on your computer and project them using the computer to control the show. So far so good. It works well and you have the ability to use a variety of layouts, colours, illustrations and so on at the touch of a button.

There are some dangers. First, do not let the technology carry you away. Not everything it will do is useful – certainly not all on one slide or even in one presentation – and it is a common error to allow the ease of preparation to increase the amount on a slide beyond the point where it becomes cluttered and difficult to follow. Similarly, if you are going to use its various features, like the ability to strip in one line and then another to make up a full list, remember to keep it manageable. Details here can be important, for instance colour choice is prodigious but not all are equally suitable for making things clear.

Another danger is simply the increased risk of technological complexity. Sometimes it is a simple error. Recently I saw an important presentation have to proceed without the planned slides because the projector (resident at the venue) could not be connected to the laptop computer (which had been brought to the venue) because the leads were incompatible. Or problems may be caused by something buried in the software. Again not long ago I sat through a presentation that used twenty or thirty slides; each time the slide was changed there was an unplanned delay of three or four seconds. It was felt unwarranted to stop and risk tinkering with the equipment, but long before the hour-long presentation finished everyone in the group found it disproportionately maddening.

Always make sure (check, check, check…) that everything is going to work and consider what to do in the event of technological gremlins striking; hand out a paper handout copy perhaps. You have been warned! Finally, and very important: follow all the overall rules and do not forget that you do *not* have to have a slide on all the time – when you have finished with one, you can blank out the screen until you are ready for the next so that it does not distract.

Anything and everything

Finally, be inventive. Practically anything can act as a visual aid, from another person (carefully briefed to play their part) to an exhibit of some sort. In a business presentation, exhibits may be obvious items: products, samples, posters etc. or maybe something totally unexpected. Like all the skills involved in making presentations, while the basics give you a sound foundation, the process is something that can benefit from a little imagination.

To sum up: whatever you use, remember to talk to the group not to the visual aid. Looking at the screen too much when slides are used is a common fault. Make sure visuals are visible (do not get in the way yourself), explain them or their purpose as necessary, mention whether or not people will get a paper copy of them and stop them being distracting by removing them as soon as you are finished with them.

Summary

There is a good deal of detail here (some of it useful beyond presenting). A lot of it is common sense, but it represents a lot to keep in mind at one time. Practice and building up the right habits help. Overall the key issues are:

Preparation in all its manifestations is simply a must.

Balancing content and manner; it is as much how you say things as what you say that determines the level of impact.

Take time; you must allow yourself the opportunity to use techniques not simply rush through the content to get it over.

Visual aids can help (indeed may be expected), but they must support what is said rather than lead.

Next, having focused primarily on methods of effective communication, we move to two short chapters about particular common intentions of communications; first, communicating *persuasively*.

CHAPTER 7

BEING PERSUASIVE

I persuade, you educate, they manipulate.

Dr Allen Crawford

Fact: agreement rarely simply falls into your lap. You have to actively win it. And you may have to overcome a distaste for persuasion to do so. Persuasion's close partner is selling and, after all, the archetypal image of, say a pushy double-glazing salesman, is not entirely positive. The good' news is that the individual techniques of persuasive communication are pretty much common sense. They are understandable. They are manageable (at least with practice). You *can* do it successfully. What is more, doing so can engender considerable satisfaction. It is always good to obtain agreement. It is better still when you can look back and say *I made that happen*.

Any complexity here comes from the fact that there are many different factors in play, and many different techniques also. The trick is in their co-ordination and appropriate deployment. Successful persuasion is dependent on several factors:

- Understanding how the process works, and how the techniques can be used.

- Deploying the appropriate techniques.
- Focusing on the other person.
- Communicating clearly.
- Directing the interaction.

WHAT IS PERSUASION?

It's a process. A timescale is involved which may be short or long (sometimes months or even years). Activity spans such tasks as persuading a colleague to join a project group or persuading the Board to accept your plan. You need to recognise that:

- The two parties involved, you and another or others, have different perspectives on the matter.
- Persuasion acts on someone to influence their decision.
- Your job is to make your case clear, attractive and credible.
- You do so in a *competitive* environment (even internally); often agreement involves weighing up and comparing different ideas or options.
- Part of your job, therefore, is to differentiate from competition.
- The process involves selling yourself, in the sense that someone must trust you and come to value your opinion.
- *How* you go about it is as important as *what* you do.

If you are knowledgeable about the subject involved and about the process of persuasion, then this gives you confidence. This in turn communicates itself to others – it is read as professionalism. Everything you do is predicated on this fact. Knowledge is power; certainly in selling an idea a lack of knowledge is fatal. For example: think of yourself as a buyer; doesn't any display of poor knowledge rapidly knock your confidence in everything that is being said?

Definition: The following may seem simplistic, but it provides a solid foundation to make any persuasion easier– *persuasion is helping people to decide*. People have to make a decision. Your job is to help them do so, and – as you do that – to ensure they opt for your own proposition.

Decision to act

Consider as an example: how do you decide to buy something? You review the choice – say a new car – and an initial filtering of possibilities quickly produces a shortlist. You decide to investigate a number of mid-range hatchbacks. What next?

You want to know something about them:

- *The good points:* Sensible fuel consumption, aspects of performance, styling and safety features such as ABS brakes. There is a complex list of considerations.
- *The less good points:* Maybe such things as high insurance costs or higher than average depreciation. Again, there may be a number of points.
- *The organisation:* In this case both the manufacturer and the distributor. Are they reliable? What happens if some fault were to appear? Here again there may be a profusion of points good and bad.

Your decision is made having *weighed up* this balance. You want the case to be good. But you may compromise: selecting the sporty model despite the high insurance, say. You do not expect there to be *no* snags, even minor ones. You select the overall package that appeals, that provides value for money and – above all – that meets your needs. Essentially you only proceed when you have an option with a good ratio between good and bad points.

This is exactly what people do with you. Your job is to

help them. Usually a decision *will be made*, the question is when and whether it will involve agreement with you. You can influence both factors.

What is needed is a systematic approach. As we dissect the process, and look at it stage-by-stage, remember that this is only to produce familiarity that will ultimately enable you to run a seamless conversation; one with which people feel comfortable.

PREPARING TO SUCCEED

If there is any sort of magic formula about persuasion it is here. Good persuaders always do their homework. A plan should not be a straitjacket. Because you cannot ensure everything will go as you might like, it must be flexible. It is like a route map. Useful when all is going to plan to keep you on the ideal route. But also useful to help change direction when something unforeseen happens.

So, spend a few minutes (it often need be no more) thinking through:

- What you are aiming at (clear objectives are essential).
- What you will do.
- What sequence you will use.
- How you will present the case.
- Whether anything is necessary to help the process (visual aids, examples, anything to enhance the verbal or written case).
- The likely response and questions that could be posed.

With this clearly in mind, let's imagine a meeting as the way forward; matters may be less complex, but you can always abbreviate the process.

MAKING A PERSUASIVE CASE

1. Getting off to a good start

The initial moments of such a meeting are disproportionately important. They set the scene for what is to come. It must be professional and business-like. Indeed, just being organised – in the sense of volunteering an agenda (one that will suit the other party) – can create the right sort of atmosphere. All you need at this stage is for people to think, *Yes, so far so good, this should be interesting.*

Other factors are important at this stage:

- *Respect for time:* Just ascertaining how long someone will give you can make the meeting easier and sticking to time will always impress.
- *Creating roles and rapport:* especially with people you don't know. A relationship needs setting up. You need to think about how you want to position yourself as: an expert, advisor – whatever.
- *Discovering/appreciating their viewpoint/needs:* Do not settle for superficial information. Ask and ask more. Use open questions (see page 12) to get people talking. Make it clear that you need to ask and that your understanding is in their interests. Note the building picture and make sure that, as you proceed, you relate back to it, matching your comments to their requirements. This personalising of your case is vital to being persuasive – and differentiates you from competition (particularly those who have failed to discover as much).
- *Linking neatly to making your case:* The early stages set the scene and allow you to move smoothly into making your case. Keep telling them what you propose to do in their terms: R*ight, I've a clear idea what you need. In light of the urgency perhaps it would help for*

me go through the timescale we would require. I think you'll find we can hit that deadline.

2. Presenting a persuasive case

This is the heartland of the meeting. You must achieve several things in parallel as you proceed:

- *Make what you say clear:* This sounds obvious, but persuasion often fails only because someone is left unsure of what they are told. And in some areas any complexities seem to be intentional hazards. Think about how you will explain things and make it logical and easy to follow. Avoid jargon. You can score points here as people love it when something they expect to be complicated turns out to be much easier to understand than expected.
- *Make it descriptive:* Paint a picture and do so with conviction. Your plan, idea or whatever – no part of it must be "quite nice" or "very practical". Use adjectives. Relate one thing to another. Create a turn of phrase that gets *powerfully* to the core of what you want to put over.
- *Make it attractive:* The prime method here is through "talking benefits". Sales jargon defines *features* and *benefits*. *Features* are factual statements about the product or service. *Benefits* are factors that do something for or mean something to the prospect. To return to the example of buying a car, features abound. ABS brakes, air conditioning, even just the fact of a five-speed gearbox – all are features. The most persuasive case does not just say, *This model has a five-speed gearbox*. It links a discovery of a concern for economic motoring (the need) with the excellent miles per gallon performance (benefit), the financial saving that this implies (a further linked benefit) and

tells how the five-speed gearbox (feature) is the reason the model delivers. In other words: benefits lead and create a reason to buy, one that can be tailored to a particular individual. Features provide the reason why the benefit is delivered. This process applies to all.

- *Build up a positive case:* Point by point you must spell out the advantages. Talking benefits, linking matters logically, explaining precisely and succinctly and giving as much detail as necessary. While comprehensiveness is never an objective, a full picture is, especially one that matches the individual's perspective. Leaving out a key element of the positive evidence, so to speak, can be dangerous. It dilutes the argument and, at worst, can do so to a level where a competitor seems a better bet.
- *Add proof:* Remember someone may understandably feel you have a vested interest in saying how good something is. Add *external* evidence – like a magazine's test results on a car – to reinforce your case.

Overall the trick at this stage is to remain positive throughout and ensure you present a case that holds together neatly. It must not sound as if you are haphazardly making it up for the first time. It must sound considered and as if trouble is being taken to describe things in a way that is right for the individual (which, of course, it should be). Referring to this will show you are focussing on them – *So, as reliability was so important let's see what we have to offer there….*

People should feel you see the meeting as "working with them", and certainly you should not come over as "doing something to them" or putting your own interests first.

3. Keeping on track

Another job must be done at this point, indeed this may need attention throughout the piece. Remember that someone is weighing things up. As you explain they will form a view of what is good and less than good, imagining a balance. So, you need to consider the snags.

Some issues will be raised – *Surely that's not enough time?* Some *you* should raise, in particular where you know they are likely to think of it and it will automatically become a negative if neither party raises it.

Answers do not necessarily have to demolish objections. They may, after all, have a point. You have to work to adjust the balance. A brief pause shows you are giving a point consideration; then there are only four possible courses of action. You can:

- *Remove the point from the balance:* Sometimes someone is simply wrong, they have made an incorrect assumption or you have not made something clear. Put them right, but do so diplomatically.
- *Reduce its significance:* Here you agree – to an extent – but make clear no great harm is done.
- *Turn it into something positive:* Literally reverse their thinking –*Actually, this can be an advantage…*
- *Agree it, but put it in perspective:* Never fight inevitable logic; you will just seem stupid (or desperate). If there is a downside, say so. You can minimise it, and in this – as in all cases – discuss the point in context of the whole balance and the overall advantages.

Dealing with objections one at a time, aiming to maintain a positive balance – and not appearing panicked – will keep the overall case positive.

4. Gaining a final commitment

Finally, you need to "close" (sales jargon again), that is *ask* for a commitment. Closing does not cause people to buy – everything else you have done does that – but it can prompt action, turning the interest you have generated into activity. The action may be to agree, or it may be some other positive step along the way – agreeing to a presentation or a written proposal, perhaps. Whatever stage you are at needs this positive prompt.

Not closing negates your earlier good work. Checking is no substitute for a close. Ask – *Is that all the information you need at present?* and you risk them ending matters (at least for the moment) – *Yes, that's been most helpful, let me think on it. I'll call you next week. Goodbye*.

Closing is not complicated, but it must take place. You can:

- Just ask – *can we go ahead?*
- Assume agreement and run the conversation on – *Fine, we seem agreed about it all; if you can confirm in writing I'll…*
- Offer alternatives – *Do you want A or B* (ideally with the first more specifically stated than the second, and with two more permutations to offer if neither find favour).

You can check out more forms of close but beware of being too clever; it is, in any case not usually necessary and can appear pushy.

FINISHING OFF THE PROCESS

No more may be necessary. If you get agreement, thank them, see to any administrative matters and end matters reasonably promptly (it is possible to ramble on and talk them out of it).

Or further action may be necessary, for instance:

- *Delay:* they may say, *I'll think about it.* Always agree: *It's an important decision, of course you must be sure.* But find out why, ask. *Why particularly do you need to do this? Is anything still unclear?* This may unearth extra information, for example, that something is unclear (with clarification there and then allowing you to close again), or that the decision needs ratifying elsewhere. Always keep the initiative. Find out when a decision will be reached and volunteer to make contact again. Action here may obtain agreement or lead to further stages.

- *Be persistent:* Keep in touch. Take every delay at face value. If someone is unavailable when you telephone to follow up, call again. And again and again. It is their timing that matters and you can get agreement by persevering after less persistent competitors have given up (among writers it is said that writers with no persistence can be described in one word – unpublished).

What matters is the success rate. No one wins them all. Sometimes additional skills must be deployed along the way – negotiation, formal presentations or persuasively written proposals. So be it. The job is to do what is necessary. It may not always be as easy or quick as you would like but, if these techniques are well understood and appropriately deployed, you have every chance of being effective.

In many jobs being persuasive goes with the territory. It is a necessary part of the job, though will not just happen and few have the qualities of the mythical "born salesman". The secrets of success are understanding the process, planning ahead and making persuasive communication work for you.

CHAPTER 8

NEGOTIATING TO GET THE BEST DEAL

If you want a guinea pig, you start by asking for a pony.
From the Internet: advice from Annabel (age six)

A business force to be reckoned with in a few years' time perhaps, Annabel makes a good point; the basic principles of negotiation are straightforward. But deploying them successfully is not so easy. In this short chapter we will limit coverage to ten key areas (some linking to points made elsewhere) to highlight and summarise something of the process and the tactics that make it work.

If persuasion is getting agreement to a course of action, then negotiation goes further: through a process of *bargaining* it obtains agreement to the way that matters will be executed – the terms and conditions that will apply (the "variables" in the jargon). Much of what makes negotiation successful is in the details and in the sensitivity with which the process is approached. The first is not only important, but also logically comes first.

1. Be prepared

In the case of a process with the complexity of negotiation, it is not surprising that preparation is key. Early on it accelerates the value of experience, and beyond that it acts to create a valuable foundation to the actual negotiation that follows. In one sense, preparation is no more than respect for the old premise that it is best to open your mind before you open your mouth.

Thus, preparation may consist of a few quiet minutes just before you step into a meeting. Alternatively it may consist of sitting down for a couple of hours with colleagues to clarify intentions and thrash out the best tactics to adopt – or everything in between. It can be stretched to include rehearsal, a meeting to actually run through what you want to happen, rather as you would rehearse an important presentation. So:

- Give preparation adequate time (in a hectic life that also means starting far enough in advance).
- Involve the right people (because they will be involved in the meeting, or just because they can help).
- Assemble and analyse the necessary information (and take key facts to the meeting).

Preparation should not assume that you can then ensure that everything will proceed exactly as planned. Planning is as much to help fine-tune what is being done when circumstances do take an unforeseen turn. Experience may reduce the time preparation takes; it does not however make it unnecessary. So, never skimp preparation in terms of time and effort. It is too late when you come out of a meeting that has not gone well saying – *If only I had...*

2. Communicate clearly

Like preparation the best way to describe this is as a foundation to success. Your communications within a complex negotiation situation need to be absolutely clear (yes, clarity again). There is a power that flows directly from sheer clarity and good description. When people:

- *Understand*: this speaks for itself, but it also means misunderstandings are avoided and it helps ensure that the meeting stays tightly on its real agenda.
- *Are impressed*: clarity gives favourable impressions of authority, certainty and confidence – all of which add to the power you bring to the table.

Additionally, clarity about the meeting itself – setting a clear agenda and so on – direct the proceedings and help make it possible for you to take a lead, which in turn helps get you where you want to go.

Clarity stems from preparation, clear thinking and analysis; and from experience. It is worth working at. The last thing you want at the end of the day is to achieve agreement, only to find it retracted later because someone says that *they were not clear what it was they were agreeing to*. Insisting at that stage can mean you are never trusted again; it is a position to avoid.

3. Look the part

This is especially important here and can have a considerable effect on the outcome of negotiating. Most important is that the profile you project gives specific impressions, for instance being seen as:

- *Well prepared*, so people give what you say greater weight.
- *Well-organised*, which has a similar effect.
- *Confident*: This can have a major impact on the credibility of what you say, especially the belief in your insistence that you *can do no more* if your arm is being twisted.

- *Professional*: Again, a whole raft of characteristics may contribute to this – from appearing experienced, expert or approachable to something like just appearing not to be rushed and again the case you make will engender more consideration if the person making it is seen in the right light. Essentially these factors bring power to bear on the transaction.

The point here is that something should be done to make any such characteristic more visible where this might help, and sometimes this might become a useful exaggeration. In addition to what is said, many judgements come from visual signals and it is wise therefore to use them.

4. Respect the people

Negotiation is a cut and thrust process. It certainly has an *adversarial* aspect to it and everyone involved is very much aware of this. While it may be important to take a tough line, to be firm and to insist, this is always more acceptable if the overall tenure of a meeting is kept essentially courteous.

Show that you understand other people's point of view. Be seen to find out what it is, to note details that are important to them and to refer to this during the meeting. Be prepared to apologise, to flatter, to ask opinions and to show respect (in some cases perhaps, whether you feel it is deserved or not!).

Apart from wanting to maintain normal courtesies in what can sometimes be a difficult situation, showing respect can help your case. If you have to take a strong line there is a danger that it can be seen simply as an unreasonable attack and as such the automatic response is a rebuff. If the strong line comes from someone who is clearly expressing respect for others and their views, then it is more likely to be taken seriously and perhaps agreed.

5. Aim High

This is undoubtedly the most important technique involved. Indeed it conditions much about your whole approach. Aim high. Start by considering, in your planning, what this means. Think about what might be possible, think about what would really be best for you – and go for that. Remember that there is often a long list of variables (that is matters that might be arranged in a number of different ways) and that what you hope to agree is a mix of them all. Consider what is the best overall position – and go for that.

Negotiation is about to and fro argument, and about compromise, but it is very easy for compromise to become a foregone conclusion. You can always trade down from an initial stance, but it is very difficult to trade up. Once a meeting is underway and your starting point is on the table, you cannot offer another starting point.

Starting as you mean to go on is an inherent part of aiming high.

6. Get their shopping list

This rule links to the fact that you need to negotiate a package. If you agree parts of a deal individually, then you reduce your ability to vary the package because more and more of it becomes fixed. Something may seem straightforward in isolation. You are happy to agree it, yet suddenly you come to other points that you want to negotiate about, and there is nothing left with which to trade.

The principle here is simple. You need to find out the full list of what the other party needs to agree. Then you must not allow parts, possibly important parts, to be picked off and secured one at a time, as a preliminary to hitting you with major demands at a stage where your options are limited.

7. Keep searching for variables

Variables can be listed as part of your preparation; listed and *prioritised*. Even a thorough job at that stage can leave things out. *Everything* is negotiable, *everything* is potentially a variable – and this includes things that have specifically been excluded by one party or the other. You may have said something is unchangeable and then decide that you need the power shifting a little on it would give you.

Certainly you need to question what the other party means. Does – *That's it, I definitely cannot go any further on this* – mean what it says, or only that someone hopes they will not need to negotiate further about something? Questions, or a challenge, may be necessary to find out. The search for possible variables and different mixes in their respective priorities must continue throughout the whole process. As the process demands more compromise from someone then they may have to accept that things they hoped could be regarded as fixed, will have to be regarded as variables. The core technique is in *trading* variables on an: *if I give you this, will you give me that* basis. And that some variables may need to be more variable than was the original intention

Keep an open mind, keep searching and assume everything is always a potential variable.

8. Utilise the techniques

Your success in negotiations is less likely to come from a single clever ploy or one display of power. It comes through the details. There is much to keep in mind during a negotiation, and the situation becomes more complicated as negotiations proceed. You can influence matters in a hundred different ways, but they need to be well-chosen, appropriate ways deployed with surgical precision; for example you need to know when to be silent and when to be adamant.

Negotiation must never be allowed to take place on "automatic pilot" as it were. Every move must be considered, and this applies as much to *how* you do things as to *what* you do. Techniques must be made to work for you and the way to do this is on a case-by-case basis – one that reflects what is right for this person, this meeting and this moment of this meeting.

9. Manage and control the process

Certainly, overall orchestration is a major issue. It is all too easy to find that the concentration that is necessary to deal with the immediate situation can result in your taking your eye off the ball in terms of the total game plan.

You need to take every possible action to help yourself stand back and work with the full picture. For example:

- Make notes.
- Summarise regularly to recap (and *always* if you feel yourself getting lost; you do not need to say why).
- Keep as much of an eye on the broad picture as on the needs of the moment.
- Keep your objectives and the desired outcome clearly in mind.
- Be prepared to take whatever action is necessary to keep on top of the situation (e.g. to pause and take stock) despite how you think it may look (in fact such action almost always simply increases the level of confidence you project).

If you approach this aspect of the process consciously, note what helps you, and allow positive habits to become established, then your experience and competence will build positively and quickly.

10. Be forever on your guard

Never relax for a single second. Even when things are going well, when events seem to be following your plan accurately, when one agreement is following another – be wary. Do not relax your attempts to read between the lines in such circumstances or assume that the positive path will continue. If you assume anything at all, assume that there is danger, reversal or surprise just round the corner and be ready for it.

Remember that *both* parties are doing their best to meet their own objectives and that the other person is just as likely to be playing a long game as to be a pushover. It's not over until it's over, and it's often late in the day that things come out of the woodwork and change what looked like, until that moment, a straightforward agreement.

By focusing on these ten points it is not intended to imply the process is simpler than it is, and it should always be remembered that successful negotiation is a matter of getting many details right together. The first step to making it work is to understand the principles and to adopt something of the techniques and how they should be deployed.

NEGOTIATION ESSENTIALS

Negotiation is a complex process and the two checklists that follow are designed to encapsulate the essentials that make it work in practice:

Checklist 1: *Summarising the principles*

1. *Definition*: Negotiation is about bargaining to reach a mutually agreeable outcome. This is the win-win concept.

2. Never neglect your preparation. Have a clear plan but remain flexible.

3. Participants must regard each other as equals. Mutual respect is essential to both conduct and outcome.

4. There is a need to abide by the rules. Negotiation is about discussion, rather than debate. There is little place for overt one-upmanship or domination, yet each must fight their corner.

5. Put your cards on the table, at least on major issues. Do not pretend powers or state intentions that are untrue.

6. Patience is a key characteristic of the good negotiator. Take your time, do not rush discussion or decision-making. Delay is better than a poor outcome.

7. Empathy is vital. Put yourself in the other's shoes, see things objectively from their point of view.

8. State clear objectives. Being open early on about overall intentions can save groping in the dark.

9. Avoid confrontation. Do not get into a corner you cannot get out of. Avoid rows and showdowns, but stand firm and keep calm.

10. Treat disagreement carefully. Act as devil's advocate, apparently looking at the case from the other's viewpoint, to avoid a confrontational "I disagree" style.

11. Deal with concessions progressively. Where concessions have to be made, make them unwillingly one at a time and trade them.

12. Do not let perfection be the enemy of the good. An outcome that is one hundred per cent what you want is rarely an option. Be realistic, do not waste time and effort seeking something out of reach.

13. Use openness but not comprehensively. Declaring your plans and intentions may be useful to the discussion. You may want to keep hidden the motivation behind them.

14. Stick with your objectives. Set your sights high and settle as high as possible. Know when to drop the whole thing rather than agree a totally inappropriate deal.

15. Keep up your guard. Maintain your stamina, bide your time. The other party may persevere at length to see when you will crack.

16. Remain professional. For example, respect confidences that are given in the course of negotiations. Such consideration builds relationships and may help you next time.

17. Never underestimate people. A velvet glove may be disguising an iron fist.

18. End positively. Neither party will get exactly what they want, but if the deal is agreeable emphasise this at the end.

Checklist 2: *Summarising the tactics*

Like any interactive skill, negotiating is dependent on a plethora of factors. The following are picked to provide a top ten of things likely to be most useful. You might like to vary and compose your own list, one reflecting exactly the kind of negotiating you do and the kind of people it pits you against.

1. Select the right starting point. Your plan should make it easy for you to take the initiative and quickly get onto your agenda.

2. Aim high, then the trading moves you less far from what you regard as a good position.

3. Do not make your feelings obvious. There is an element of bluff. If your face and body language say "this is minor" as you respond to something major you will do better.

4. Use silence. Some things demand no reaction at all.

5. Watch for early difficulty. Let a rapport and momentum build up before you tackle contentious issues.

6. Do not exaggerate facts. They can be verified and exaggeration causes problems later.

7. Communicate clearly. Remember the need for understanding as a foundation to the whole process.

8. Be seen to go with the other person's way of doing things, at least to some degree and particularly if you are on their ground.

9. Do not push too hard. There is usually a line beyond which the outcome is not a better deal, but complete breakdown.

10. When negotiation is finished, stop. Once agreement is reached, clear, agreed and perhaps noted, move on to other matters. Otherwise people may say: *I've been thinking...* and you are back to square one.

The importance of different factors like these depends on the nature of the negotiation. Something full of complex financial details poses different problems from something simpler.

Finally, you should note a few things to *avoid*. You will only excel if you never:

1. Over-react if responses are negative; the other person is at pains not to say how excellent every point is

2. Allow yourself to become over-emotional, unpleasant, provocative or insulting; a planned and controlled display of emotion may be useful, but you must know what you are doing

3. Agree to something you do not want; in many situations there is a minimal deal, which your plan should identify, below which it is better to walk away.

Sometimes one key factor influences things disproportionately. For example, a sponsorship deal was once being negotiated by a famous American sportsman with a sports clothing manufacturer. His face would be used in promotion, he would make some appearances and they would pay him well during the period that the deal ran. He wanted more money than the company wanted to pay. They wanted an agreement fast to use the arrangement in a new product launch, already scheduled. By agreeing to the man's face being used in this one-off campaign, for a reasonable fee, while overall negotiations continued, the sport's agent put the man in a very strong position – as the launch broke and his face appeared across the nation the company realised that they either had to agree terms or explain to the public why he was no longer "the face of the product". Smart agent; or perhaps a lapse of concentration by the company people fronting the negotiation? No matter, the interaction of timing and money were instrumental in settling the deal.

This kind of situation is just as common in less high-profile business situations. Again it emphasises the need for preparation and keeping track of things as negotiation proceeds and above all doing so in an organised way.

Every negotiating situation you face can teach you something: what works well, what should be avoided, what best fits your style. The detail is important. Sometimes what makes the difference between success and failure is small and seemingly insignificant. One phrase, even one gesture may make such a difference. If all the details are right, the whole will be more likely to work well.

Negotiation, or rather well-handled negotiation, can be very useful. When push comes to shove, a considered and careful – indeed watchful – approach, systematically applied is probably best; and remember the saying attributed to Lord Hore-Belisha:

When a man tells me he is going to put all his cards on the table, I always look up his sleeve.

This sentiment should be regarded as good advice by any good negotiator.

Note: Negotiation, another title in this Smart Skills series, written by Anthony Jack, goes into more detail.

AFTERWORD

We cannot ensure success, but we can deserve it.
John Adams (US President)

There is an old saying that there is no such thing as a minor detail; all details are major. This is certainly true of communications. Success, or failure, may occur – or be made more or less likely – by small changes. If these pages have demonstrated anything then it is surely that.

To return to a danger identified early on, the greatest likelihood of communications failure comes not from major errors, but rather from inattention, lack of preparation and lack of thought; an assumption that there will be no problem and that you can wing it. Rarely is this so. Communication, especially of anything inherently posing any sort of problem or difficulty, needs working at. But doing so is eminently worthwhile.

Good, powerful communication:

- *Makes things happen*. It prompts discussion, consideration and decision and may help you influence action, events and get your own way.
- *Impresses*. How you communicate is a key part of your profile, and if this is positive it too helps you achieve things both in your work and in your career.

Communication must be made to work. The penalties of failure are many and can be serious – but the opportunities, what was described earlier as "an open goal", are often *very* considerable. No one, however much the focus of their job is on other, perhaps more technical, matters should ignore this area. It is a key to many successes. Whatever you communicate by whatever means – *you make it happen*. Thus you must *plan to make it happen*. You can rarely, if ever, 'just wing it'; it needs care in preparation and in execution. Given appropriate consideration you *can* make it go well.